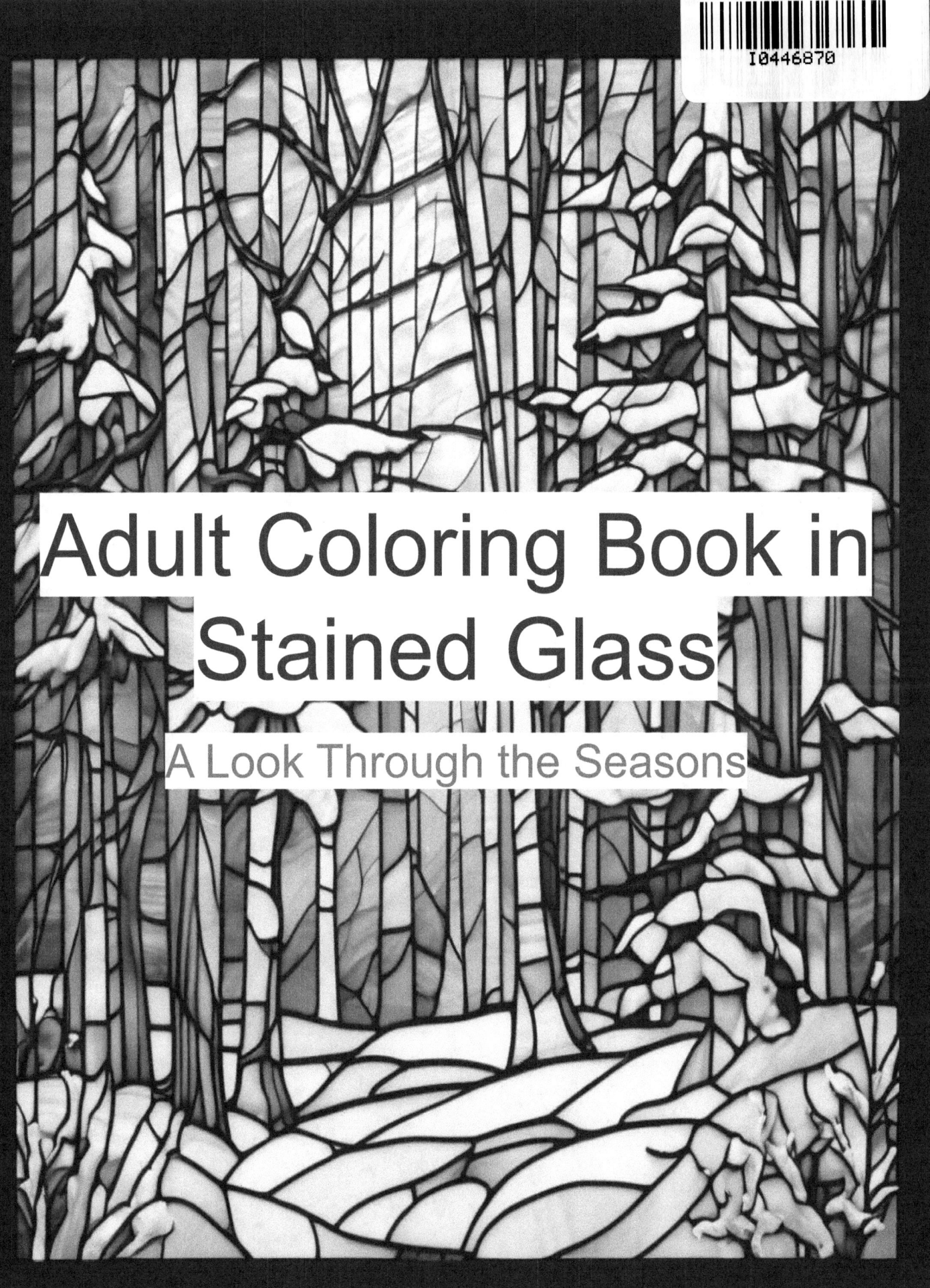

Adult Coloring Book in Stained Glass

A Look Through the Seasons

K. L. Mack

January

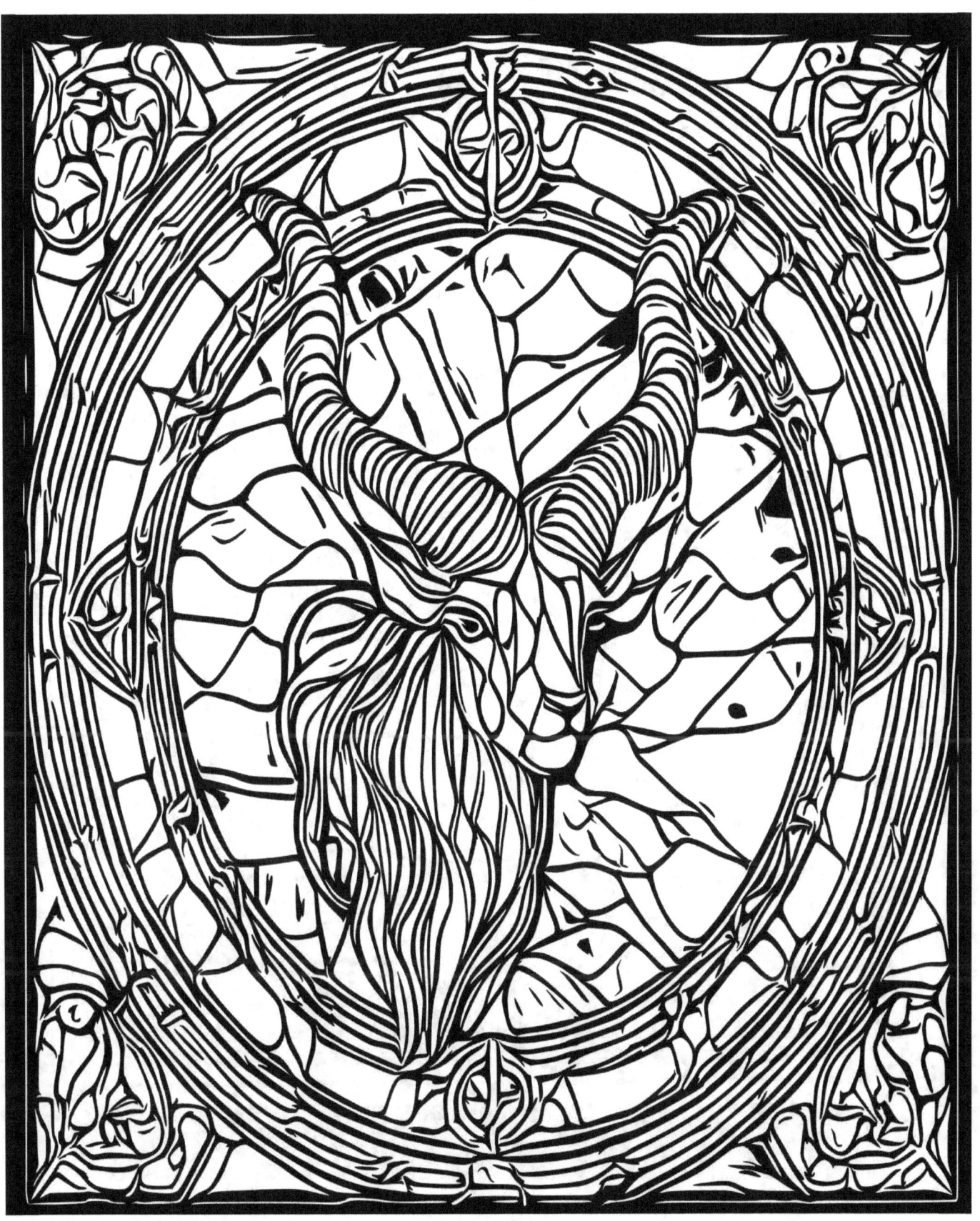

Capricorn

January

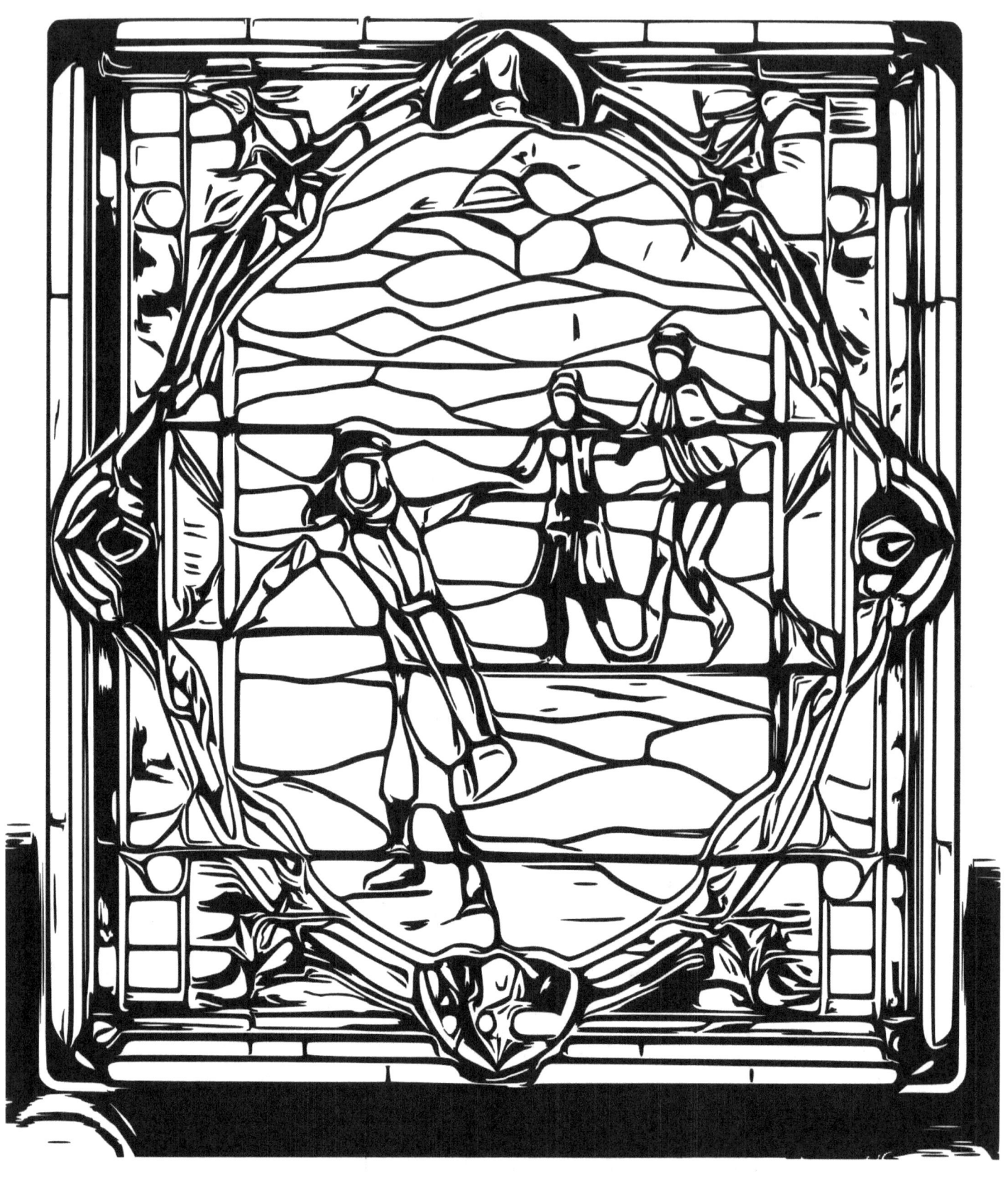

Ice Skating on the Pond

January

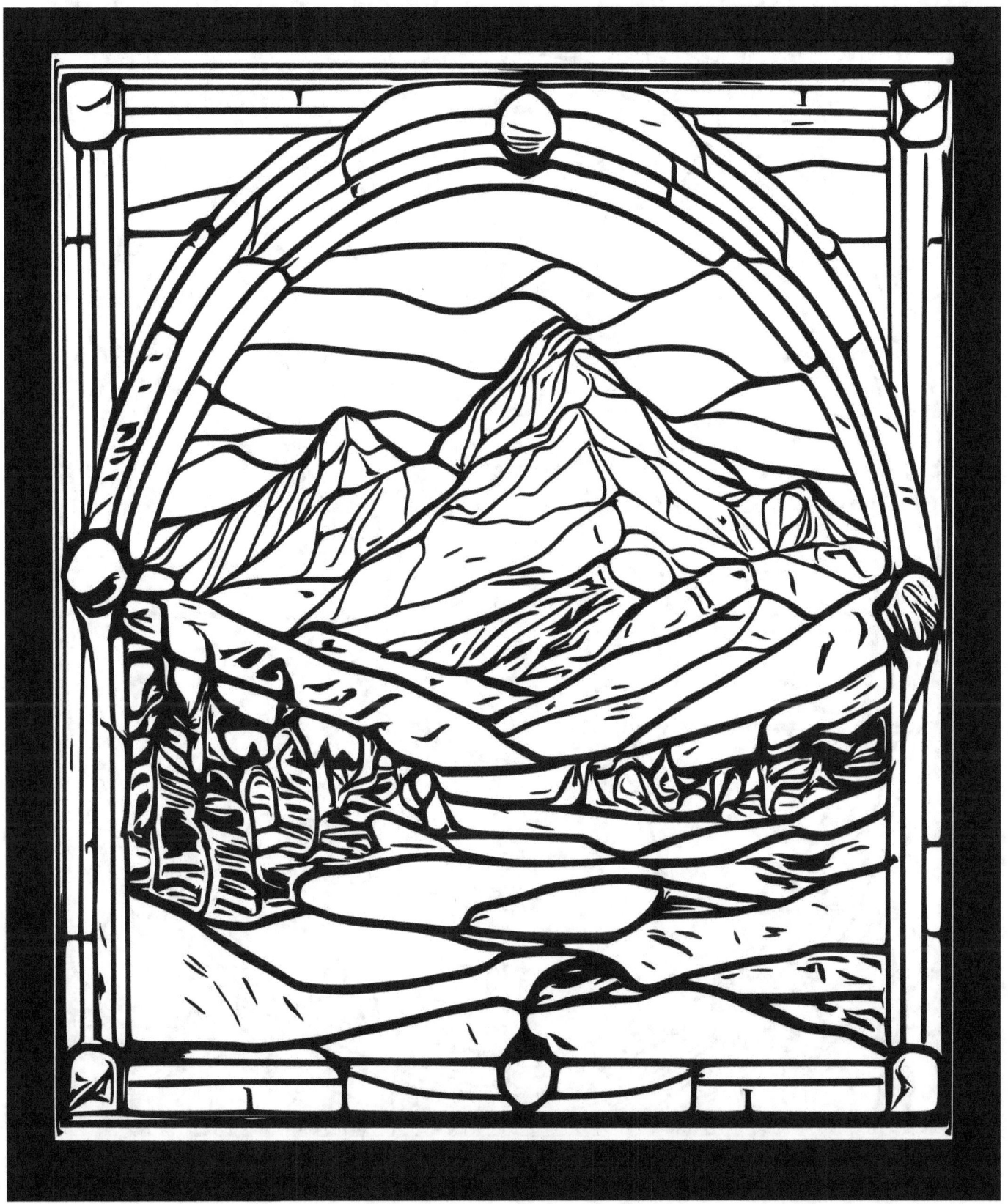

Snowy Mountain Landscape

January

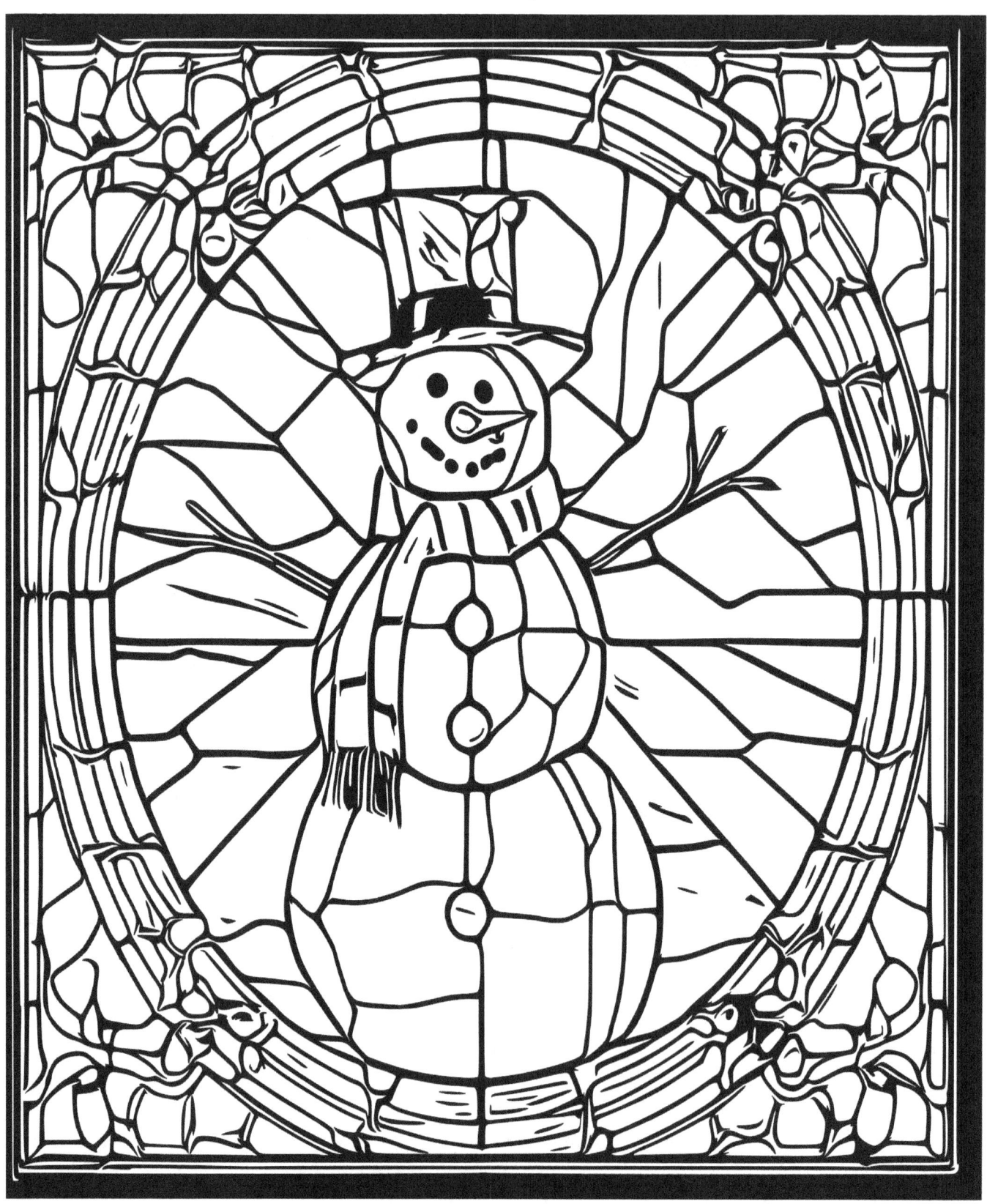

Building a Snowman

January

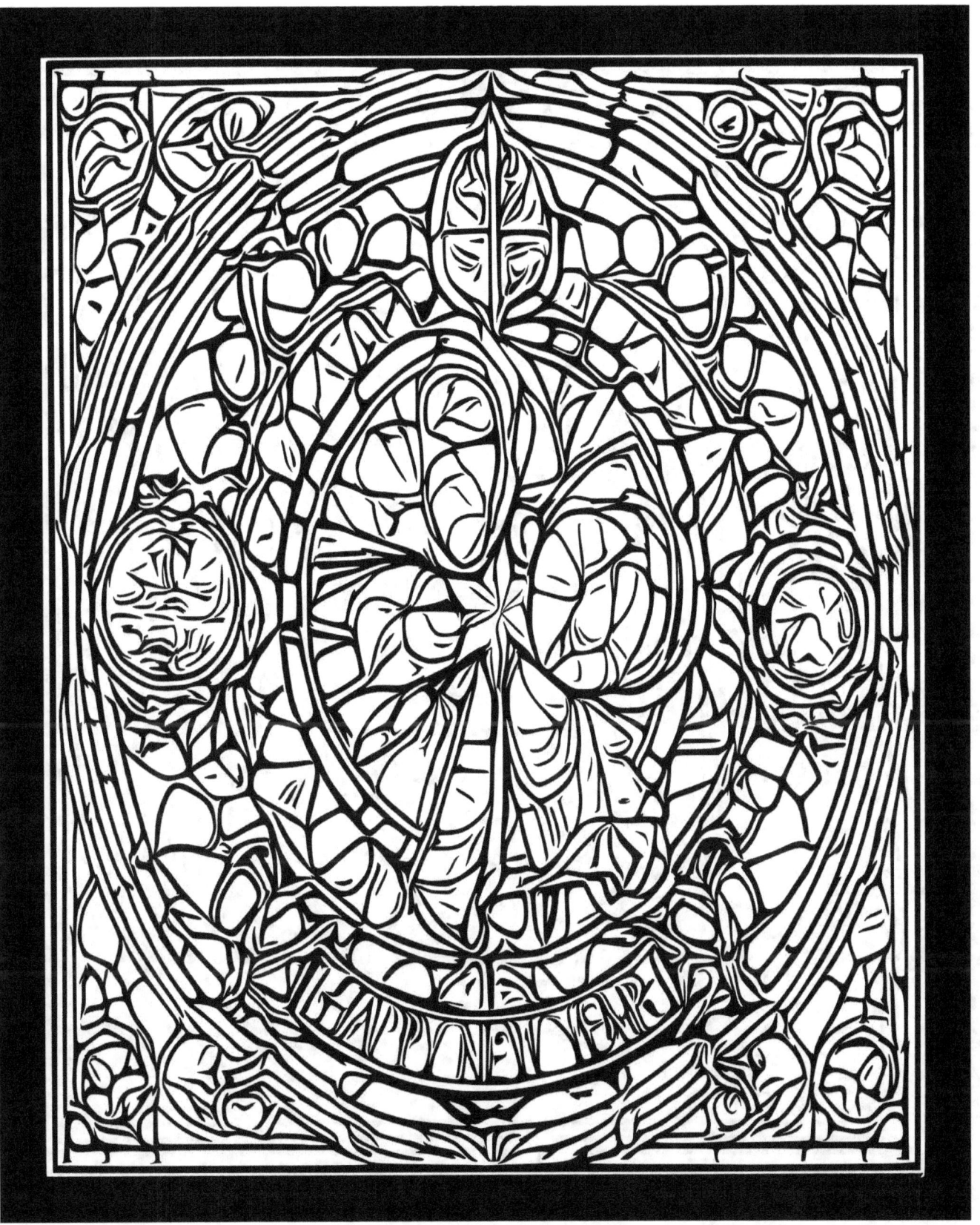

Happy New Year

January

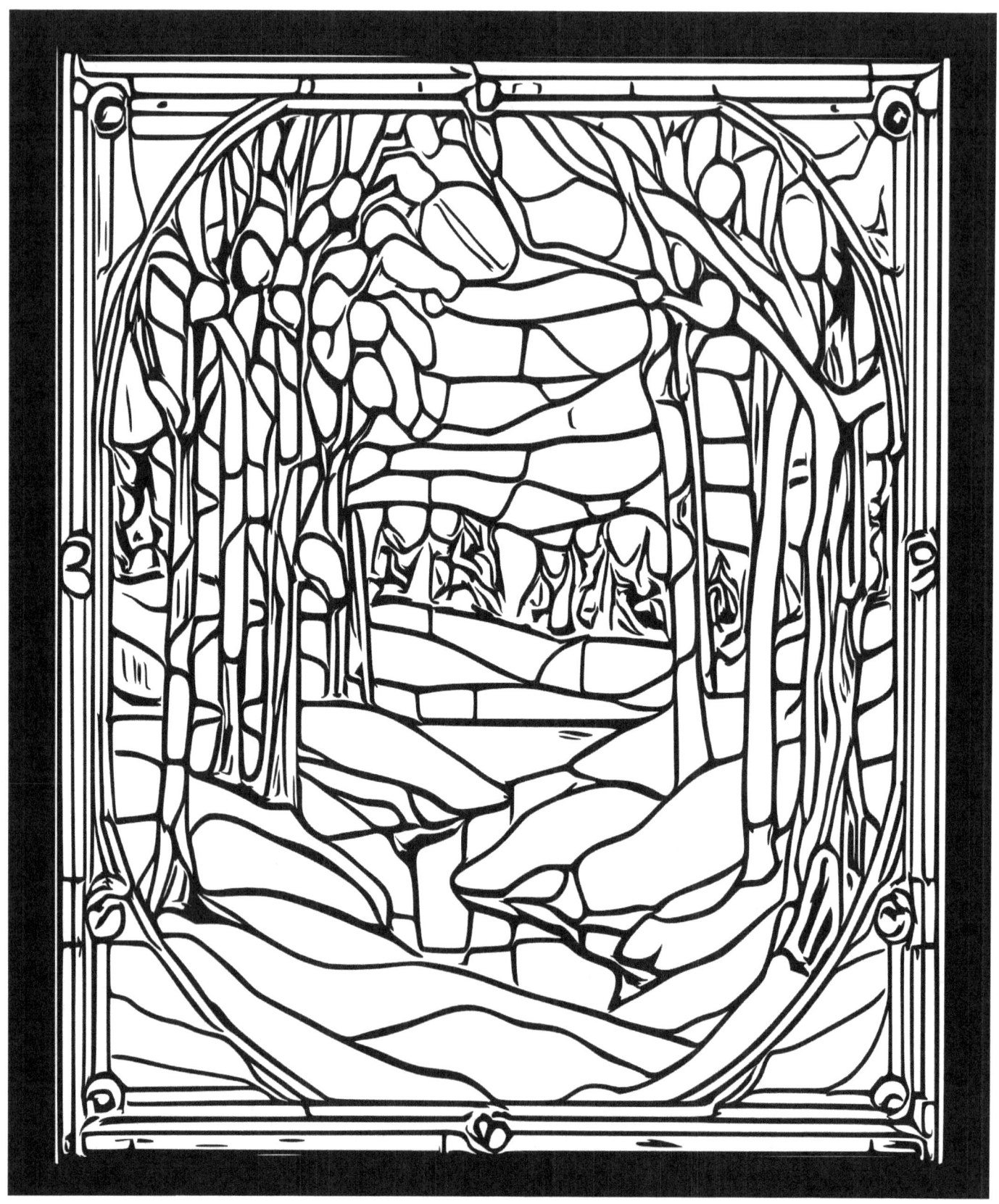

Frozen River Through Snow Covered Forest

January

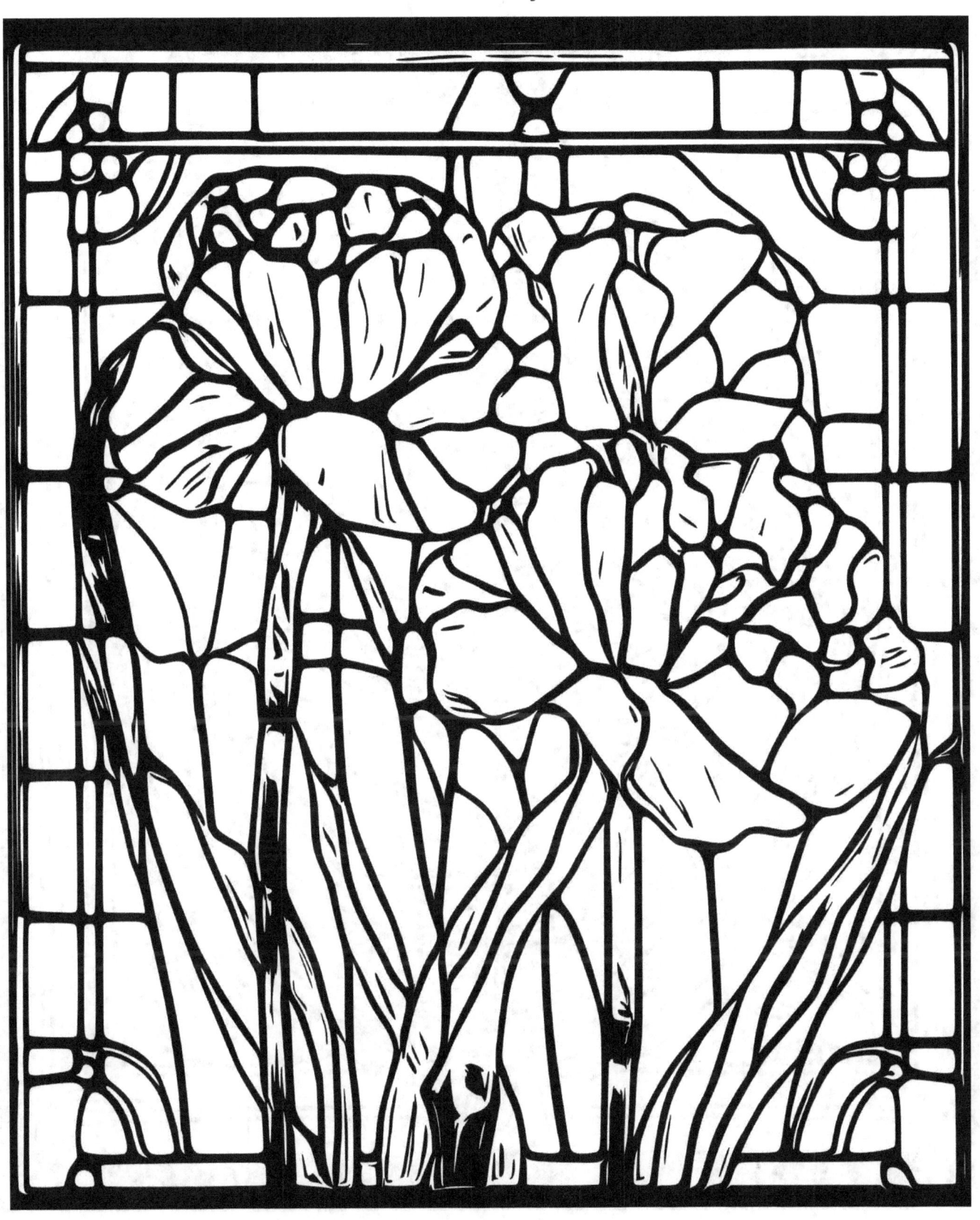

Flower of the Month: Carnation

February

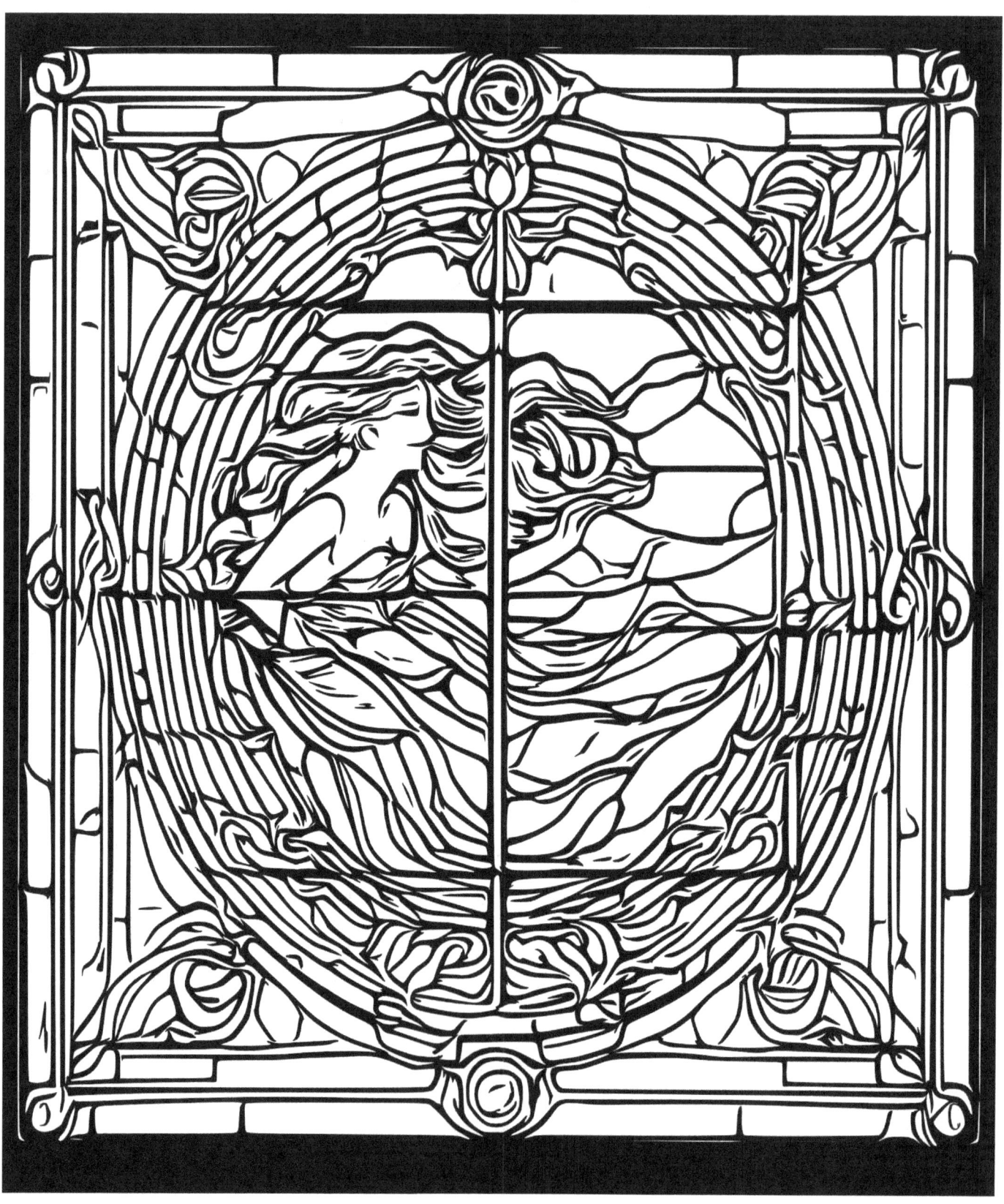

Aquarius

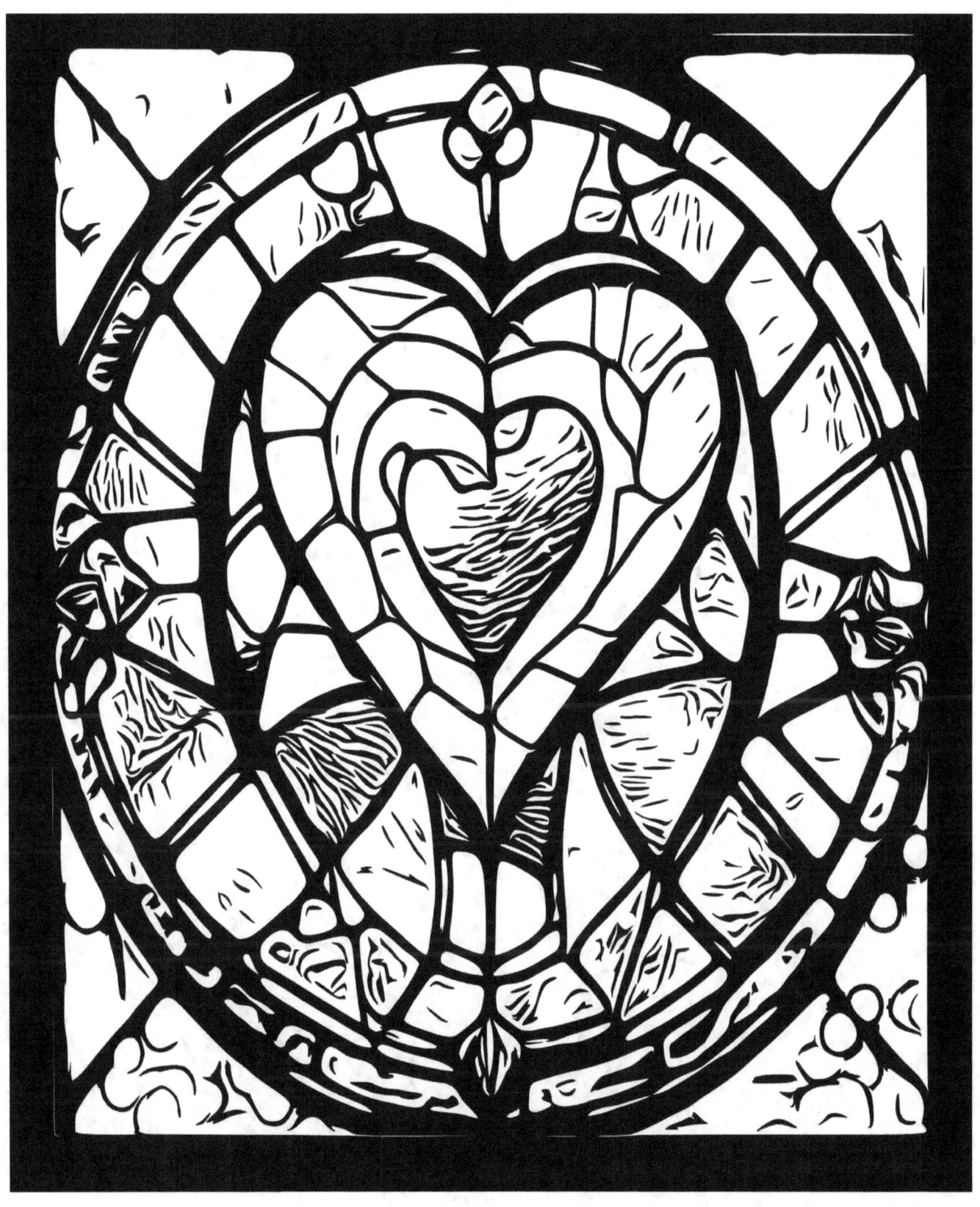

Will you be my Valentine?

February

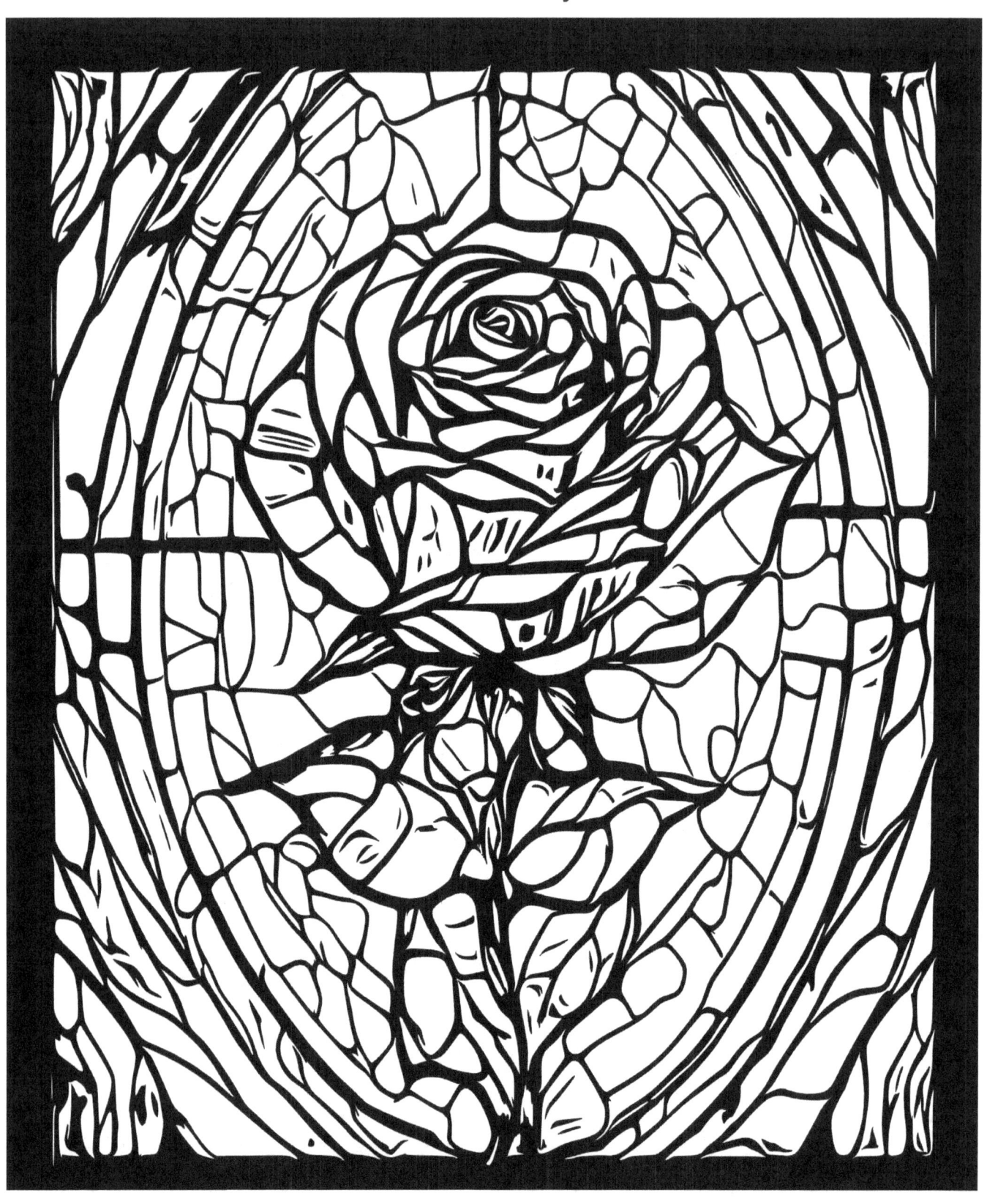

A Rose for My True Love

February

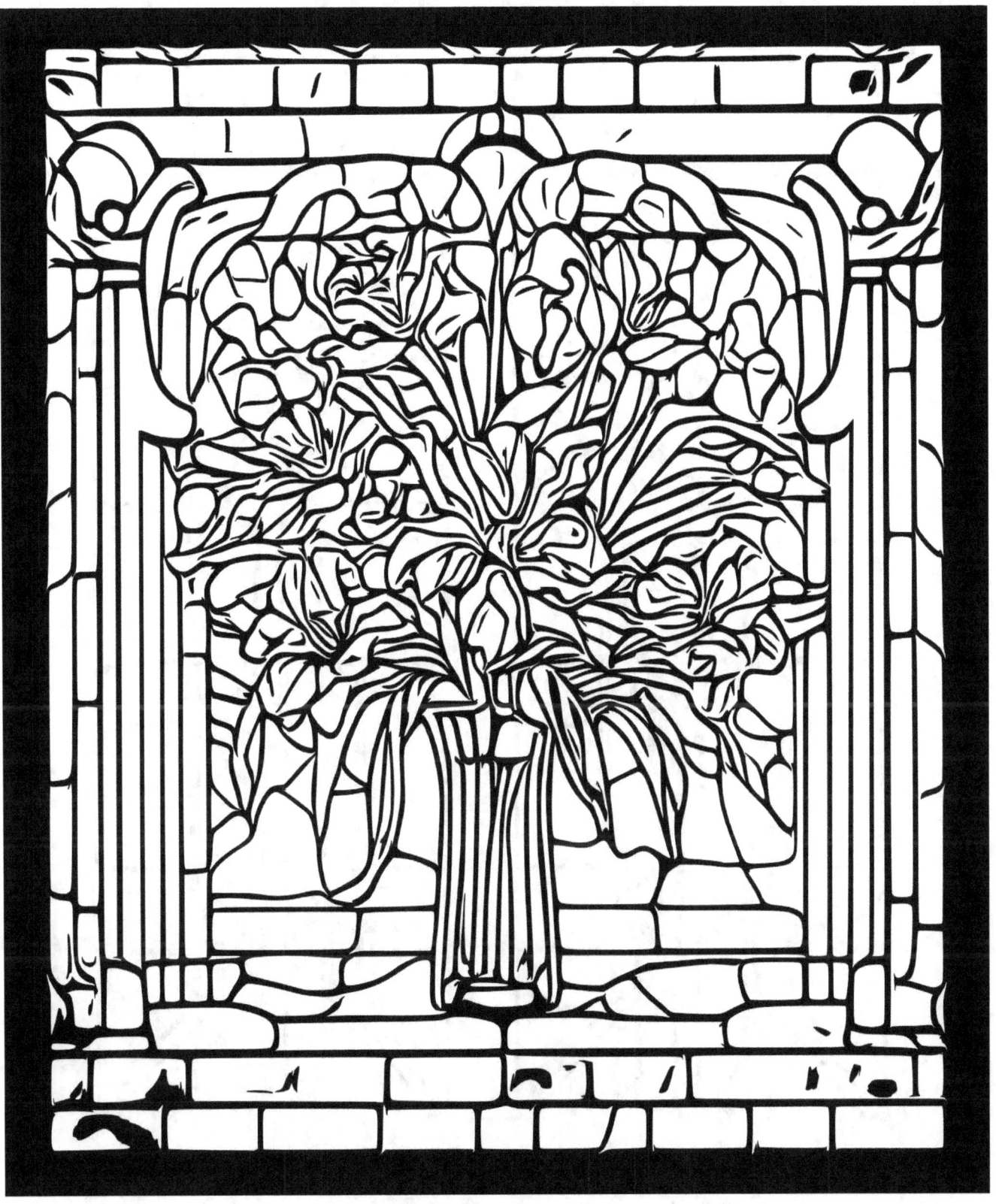

Bouquet

February

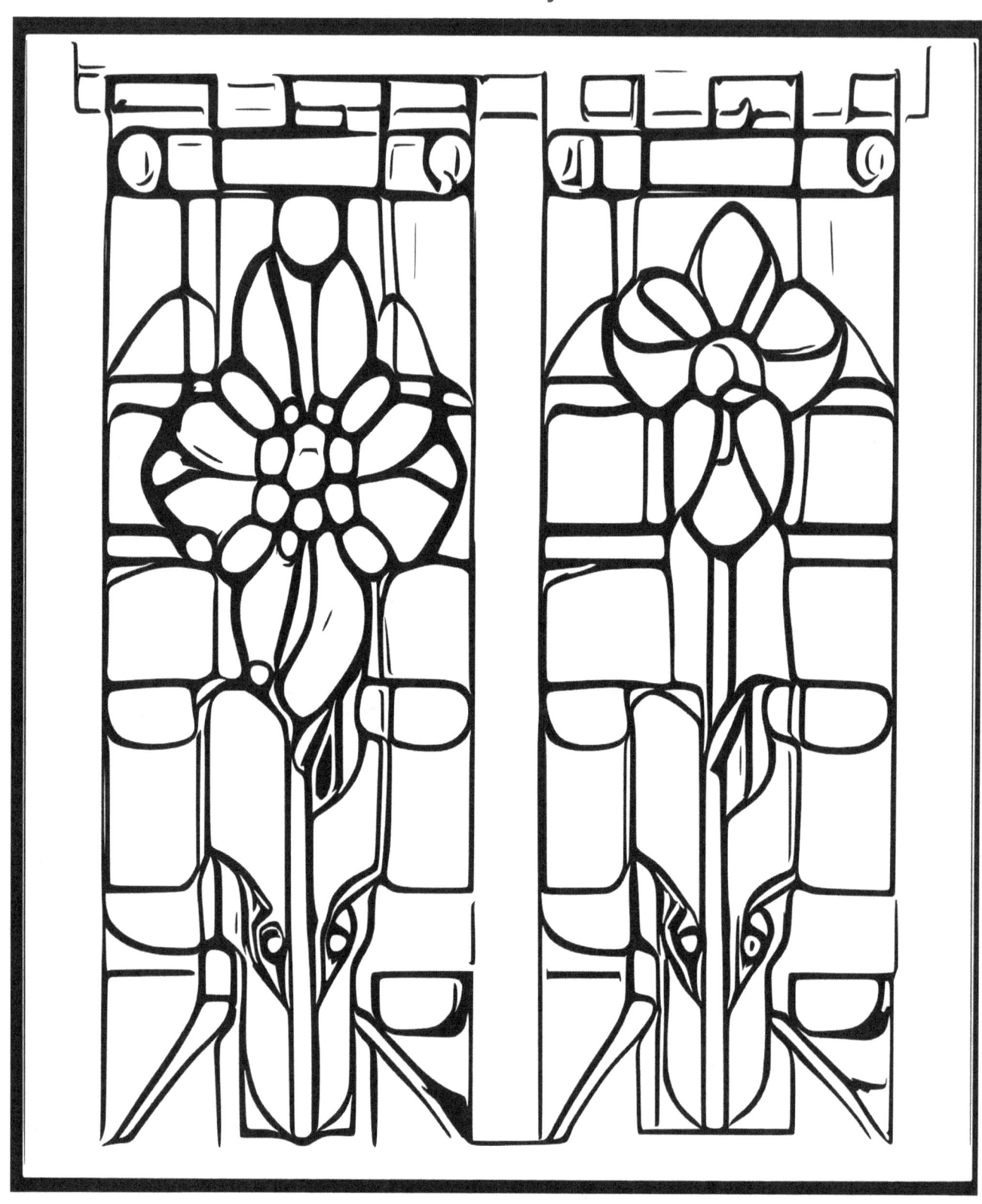

Flower of the Month: Violet and Primrose

March

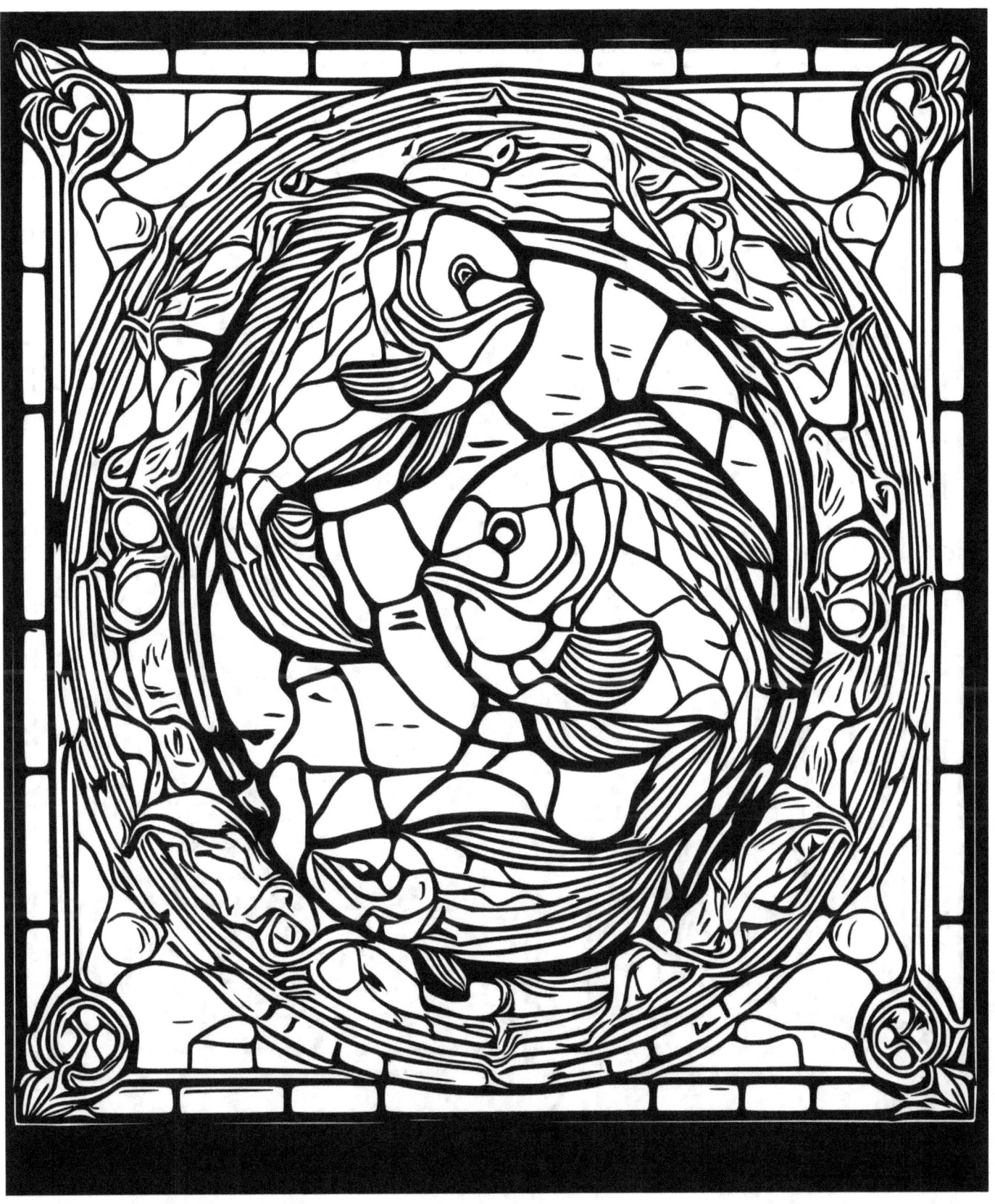

Pisces

March

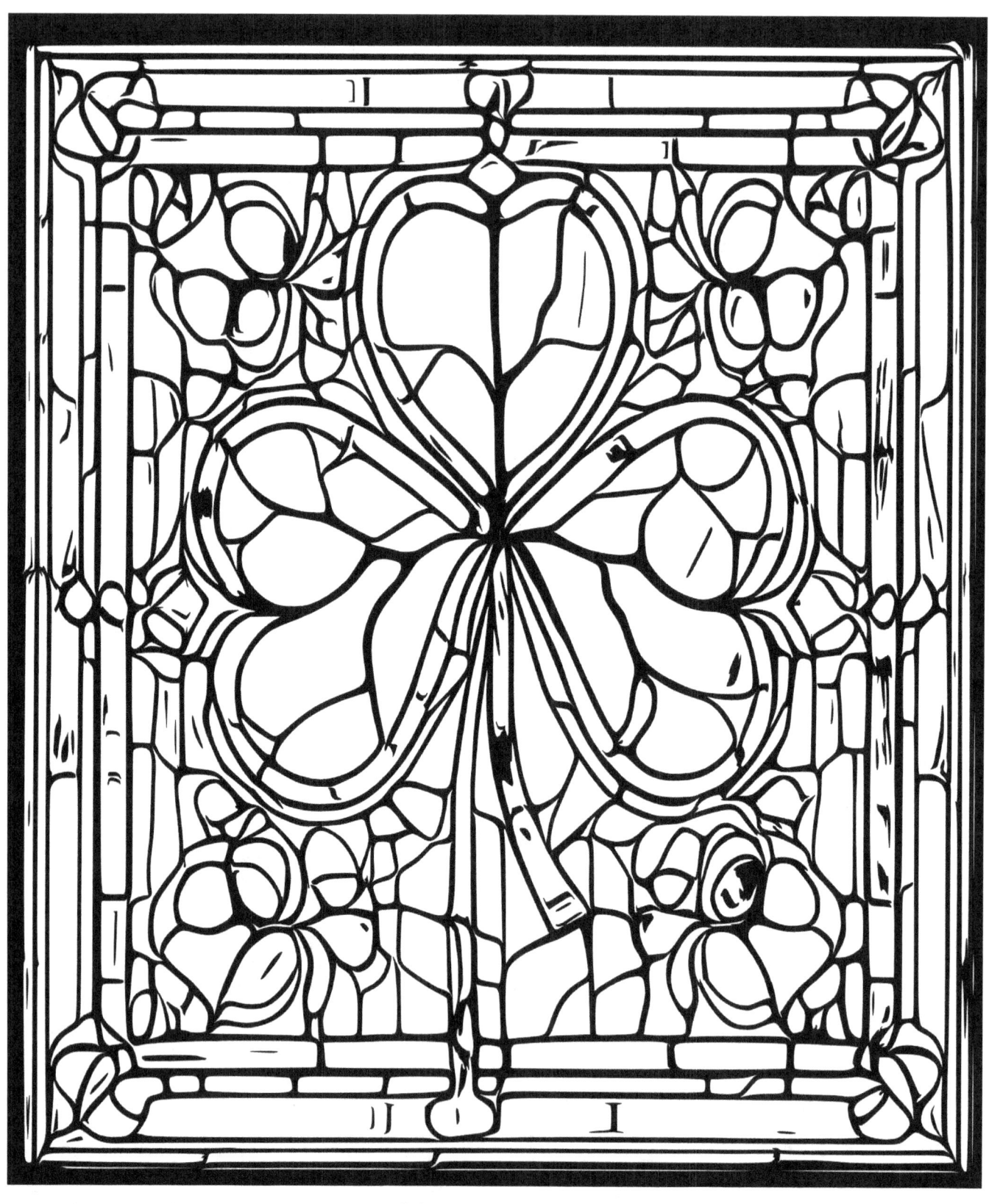

Shamrock

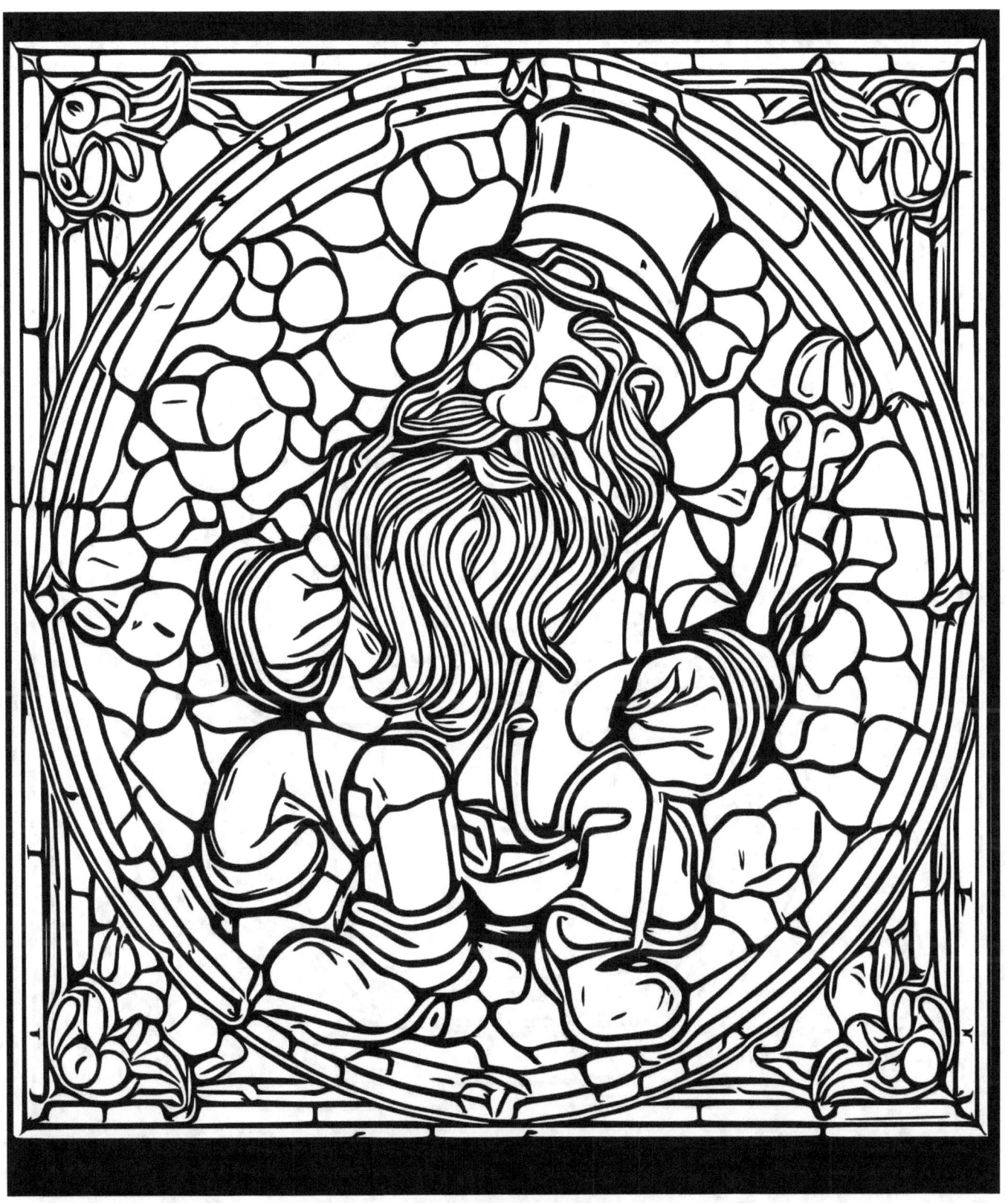

Leprechaun

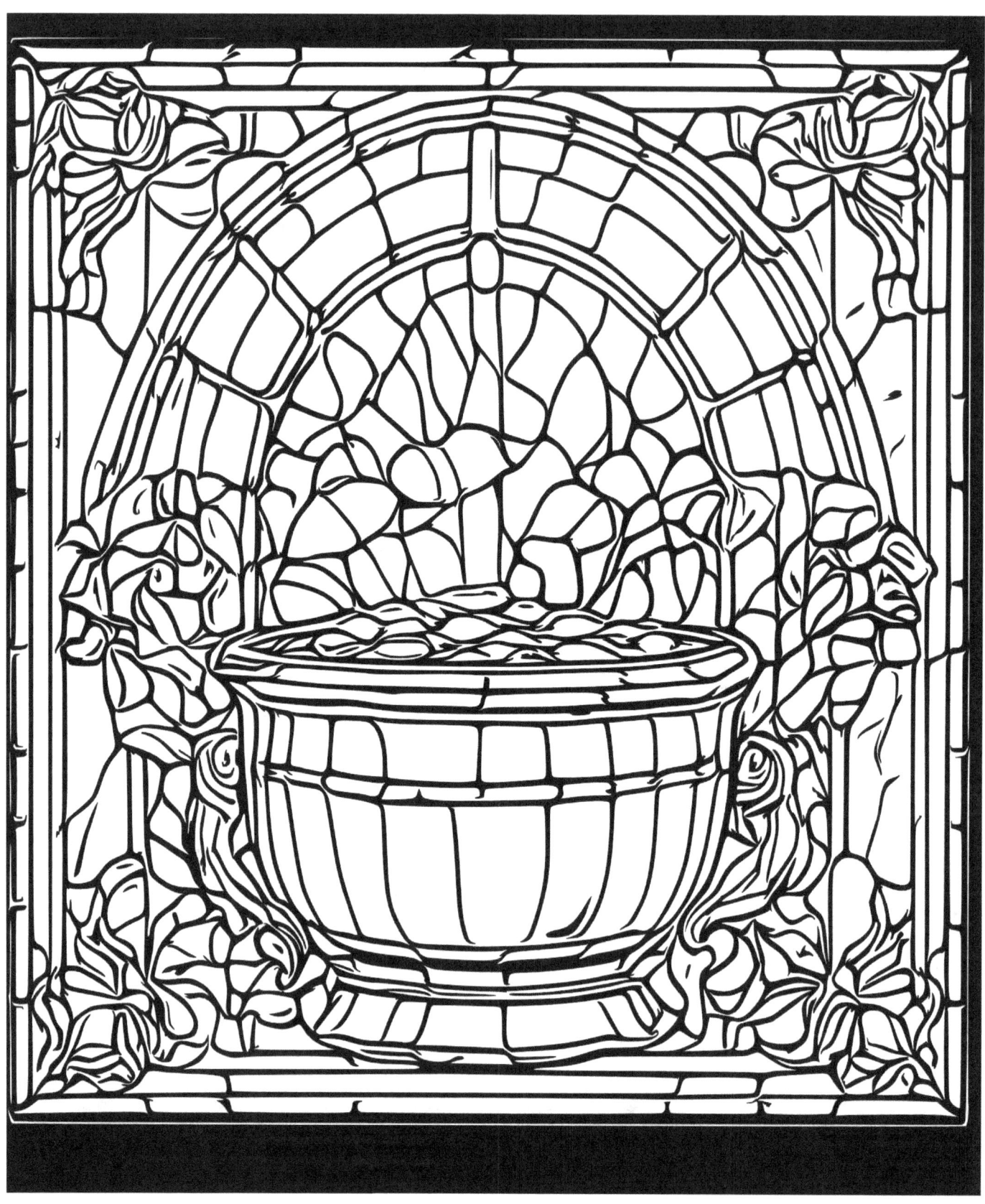

Pot of Gold

March

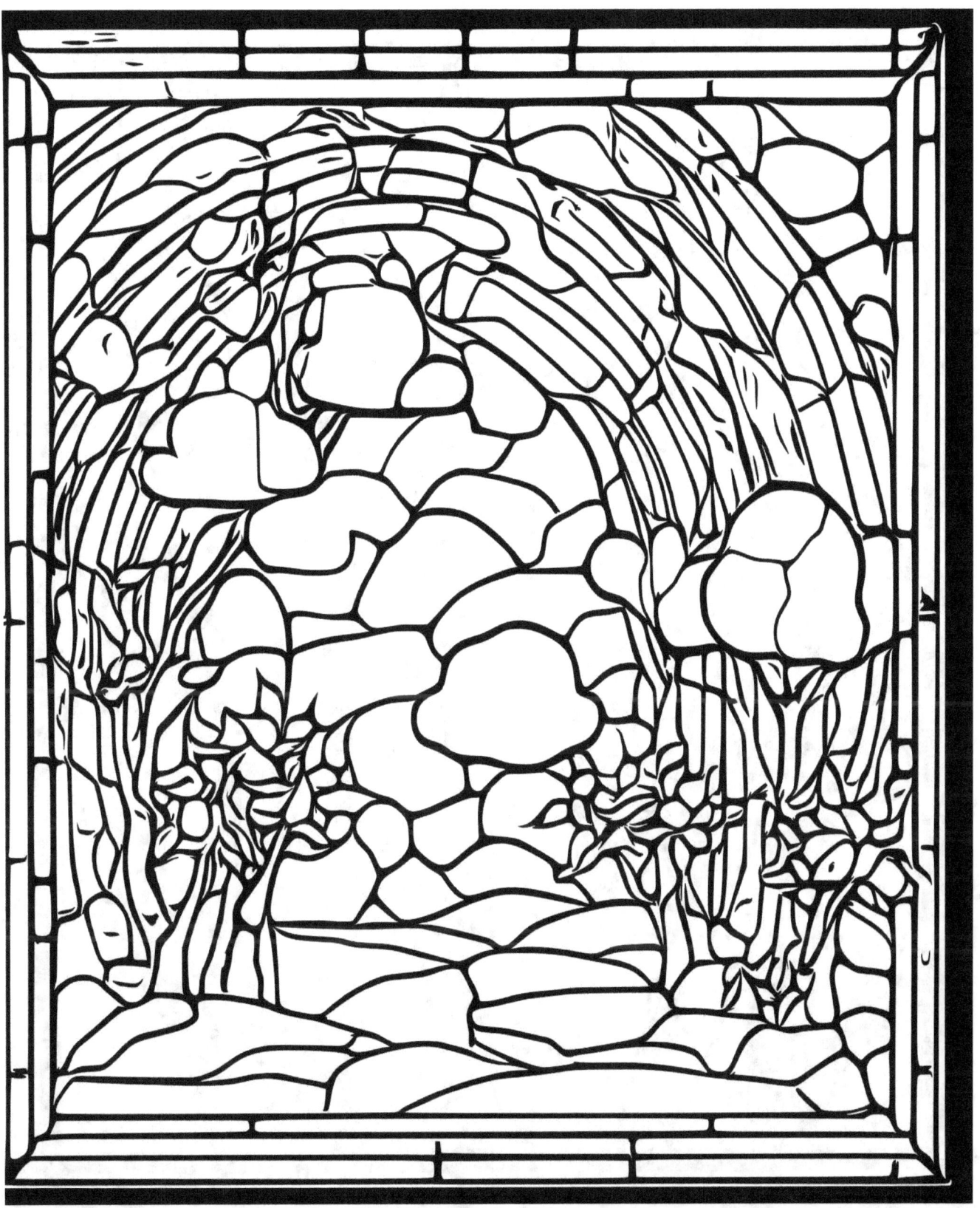

Follow the Rainbow to the Gold

March

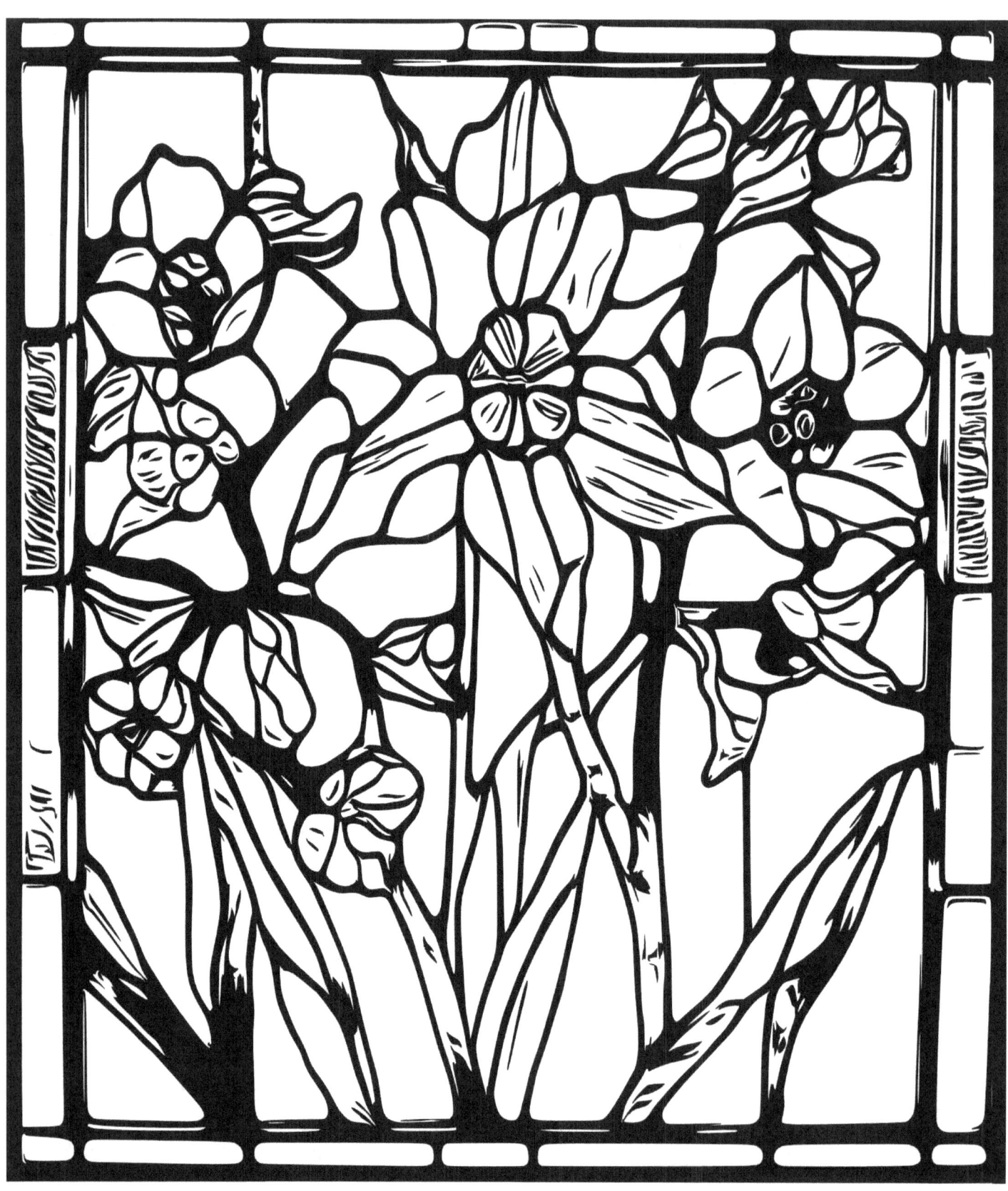

Flower of the Month: Daffodil

April

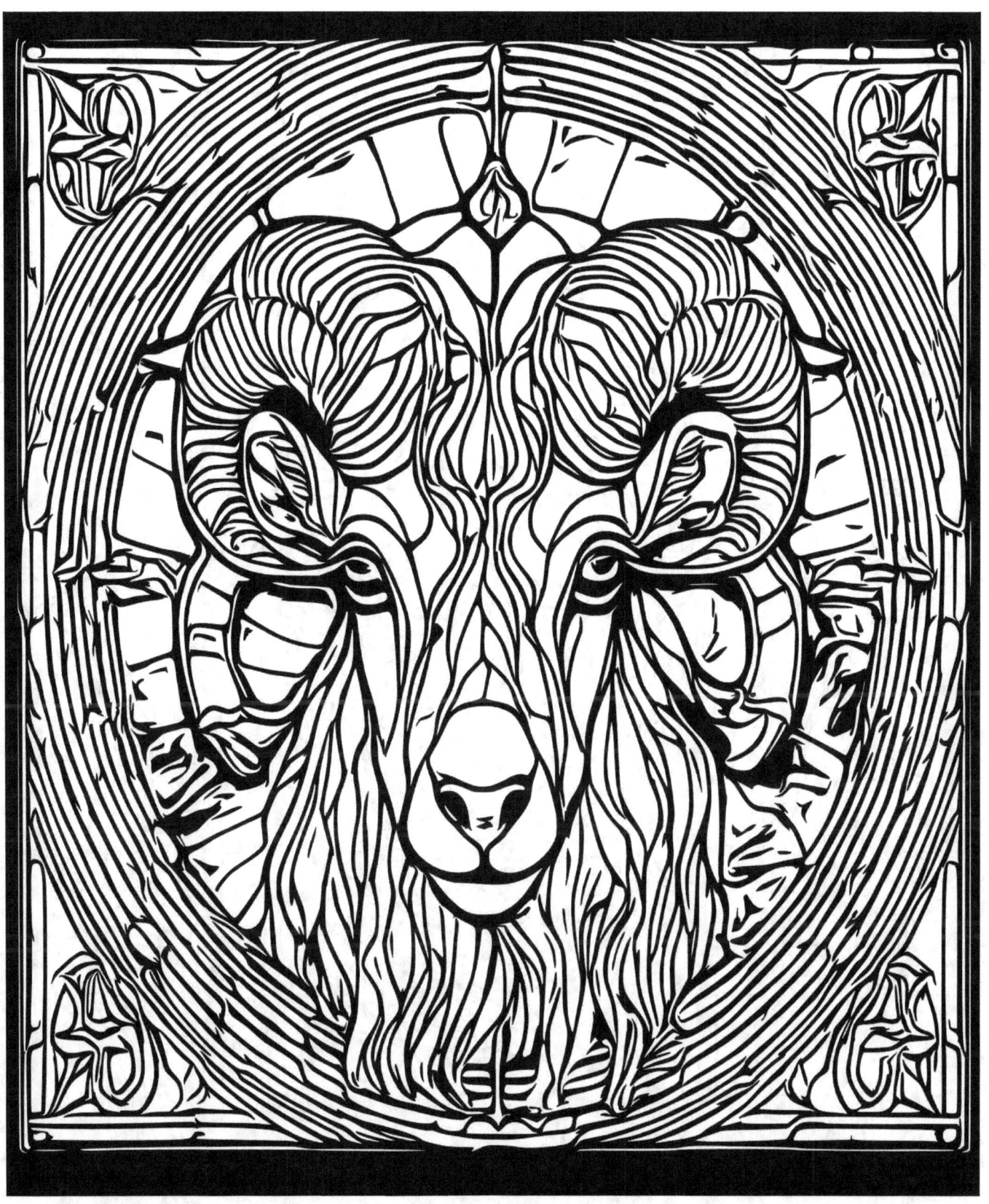

Aries

April

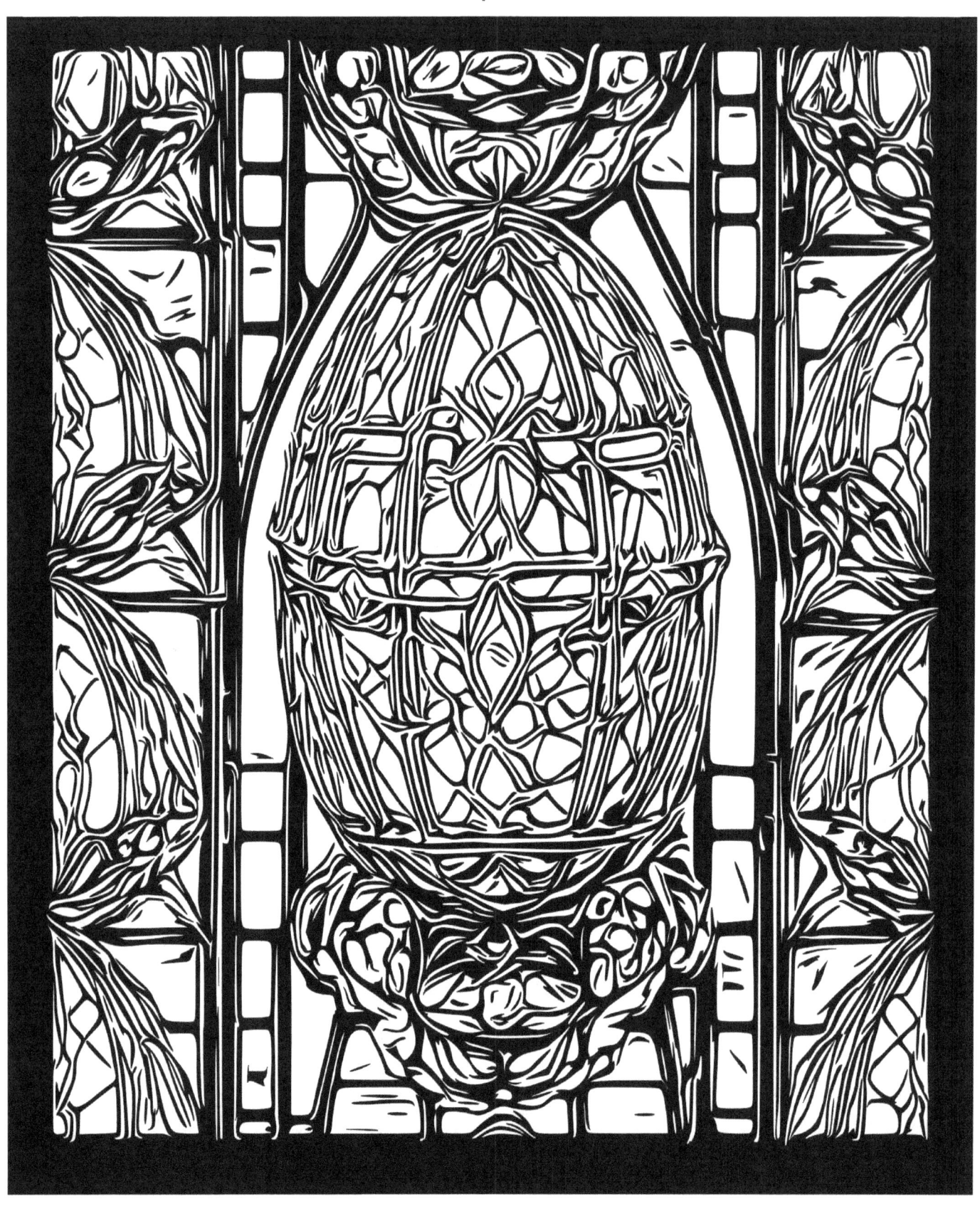

Faberge Egg

April

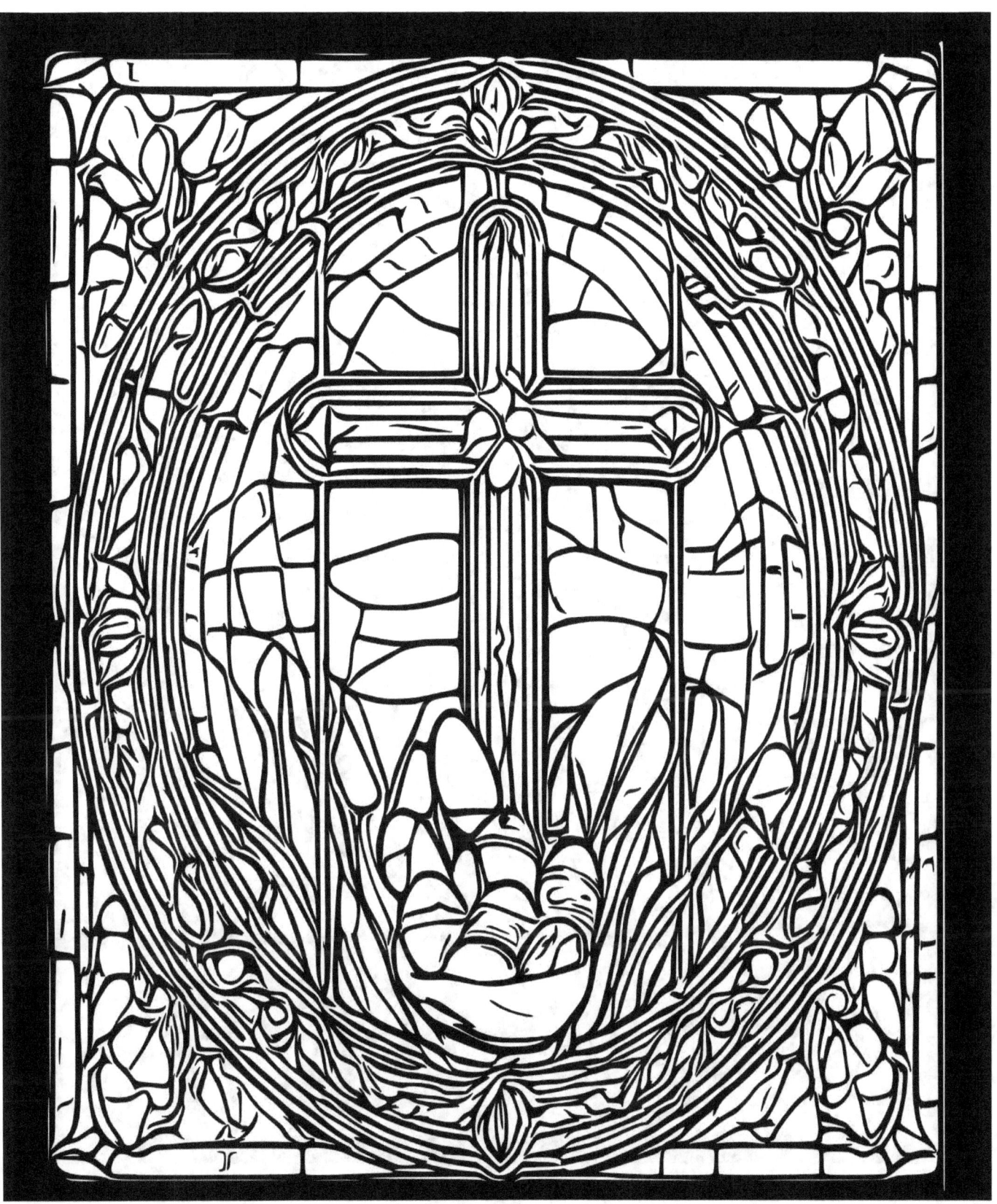

Easter

April

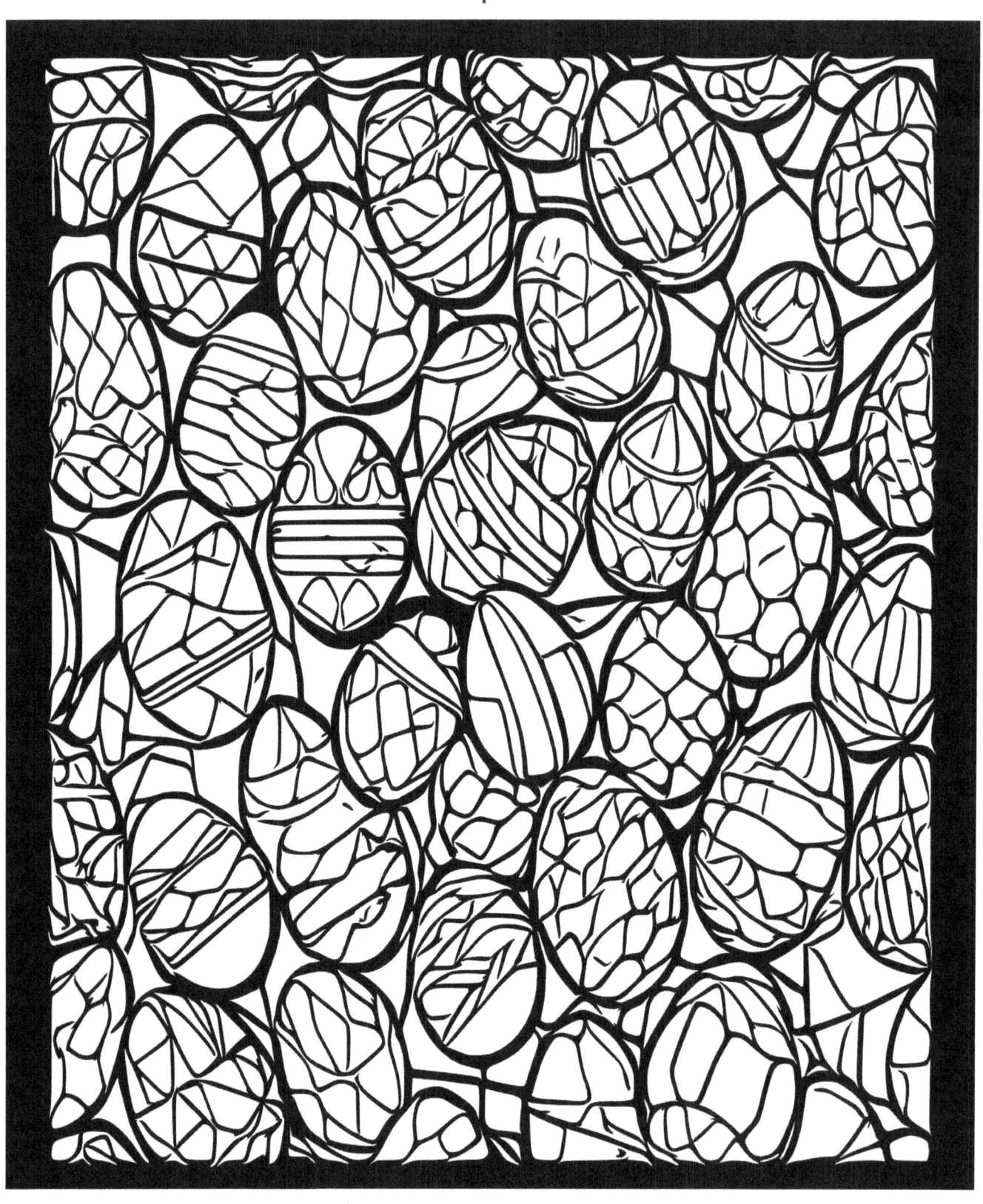

Easter Egg Hunt

April

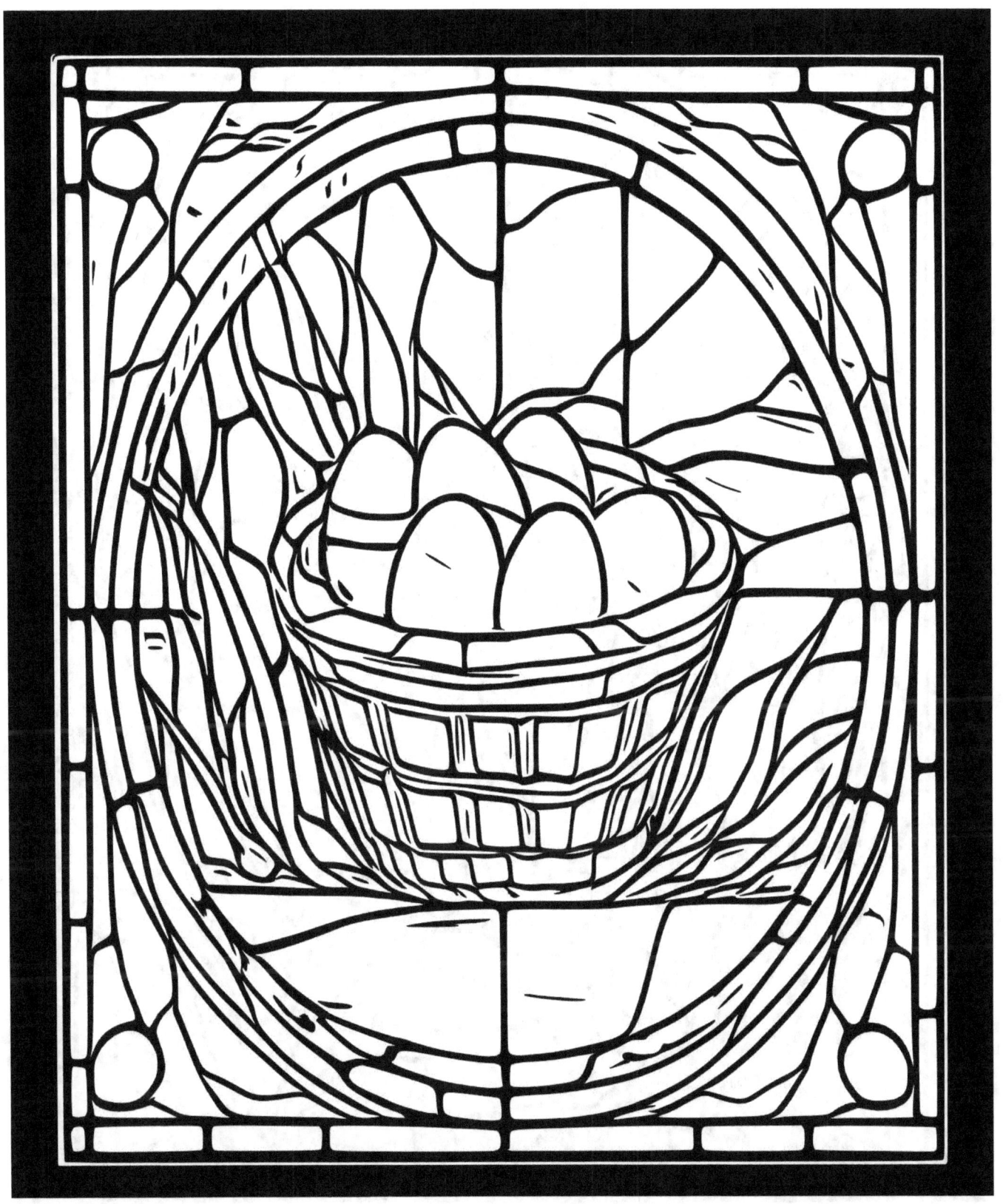

Easter Basket

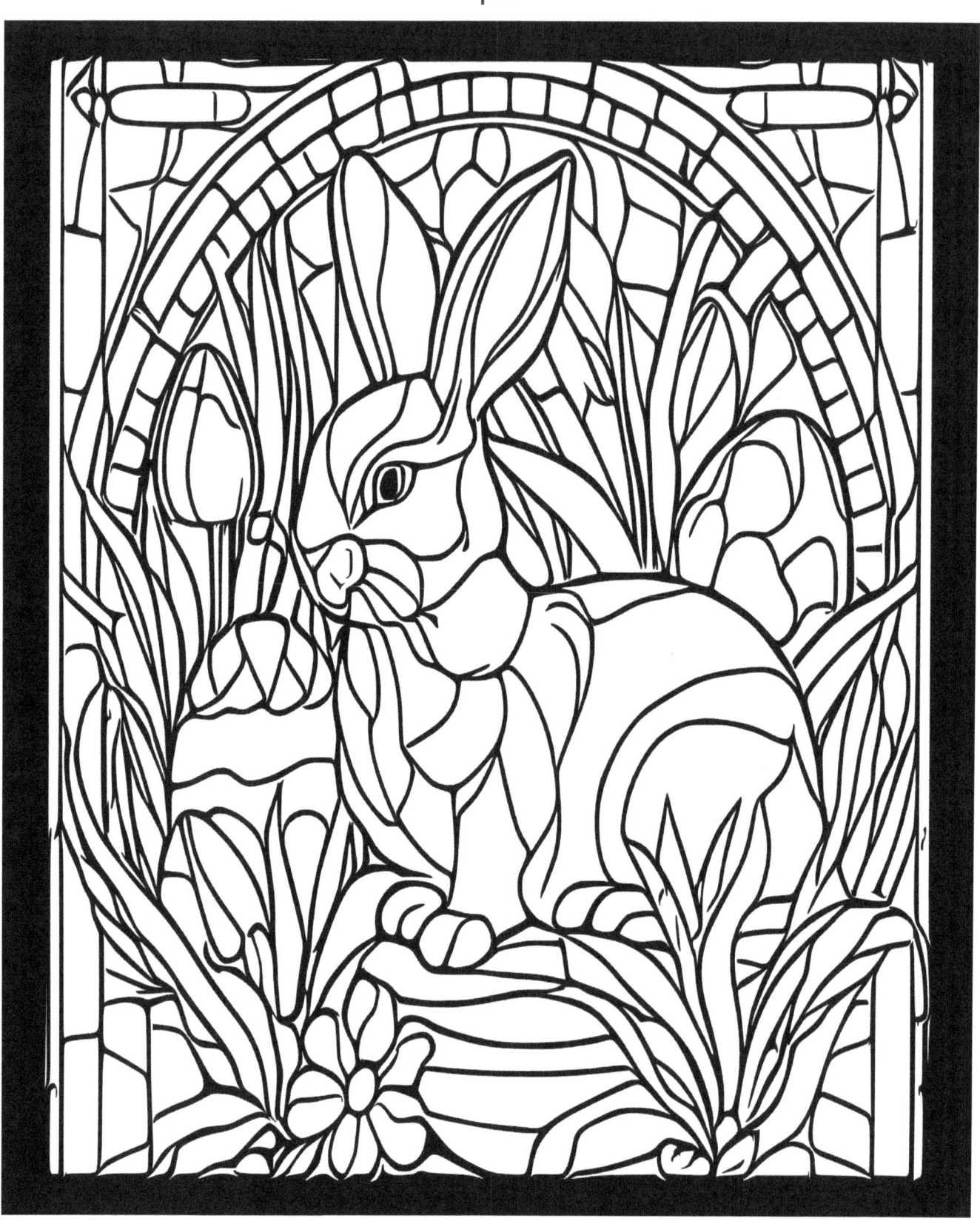

Bunny and Eggs

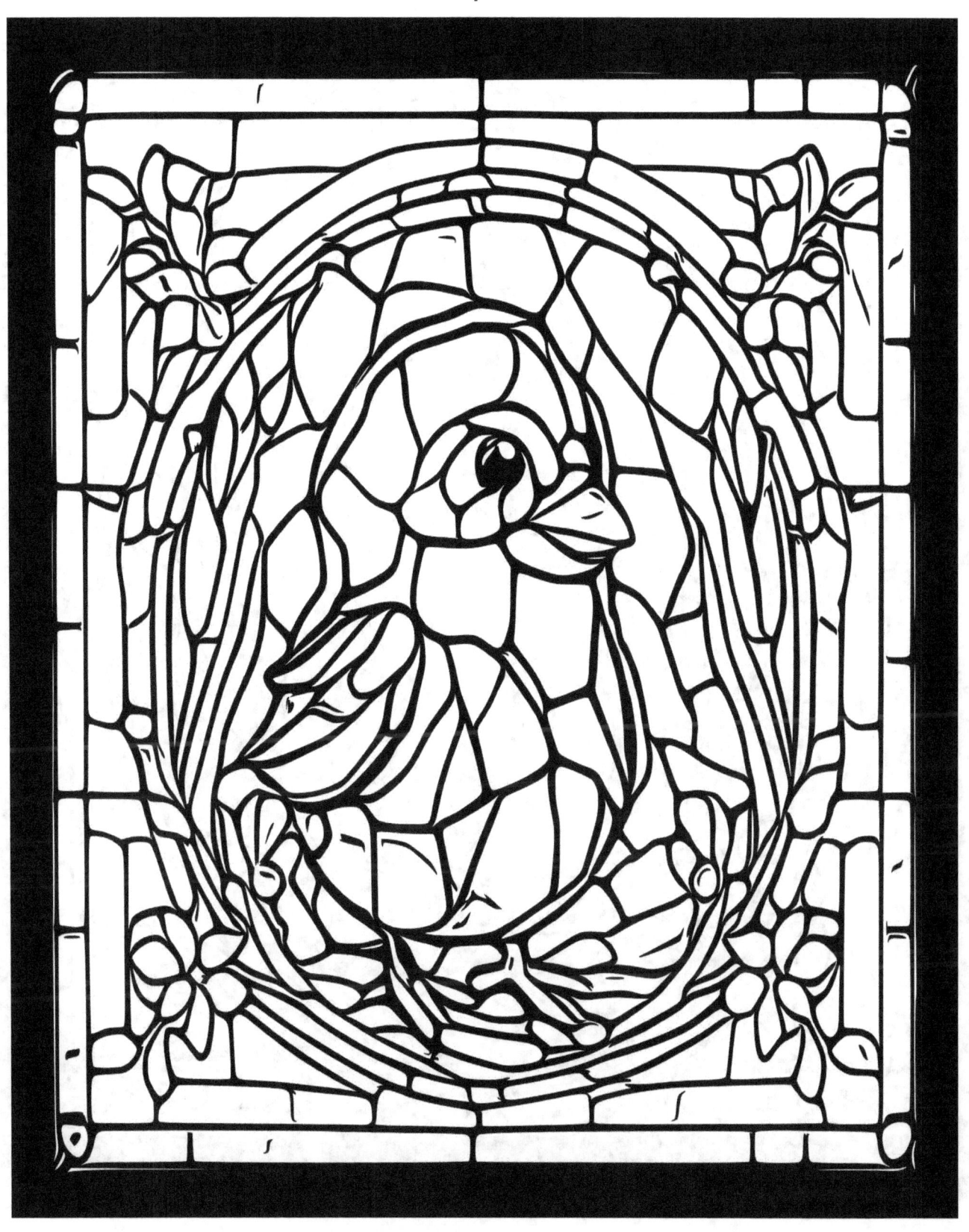

Baby Chick in a Vest

April

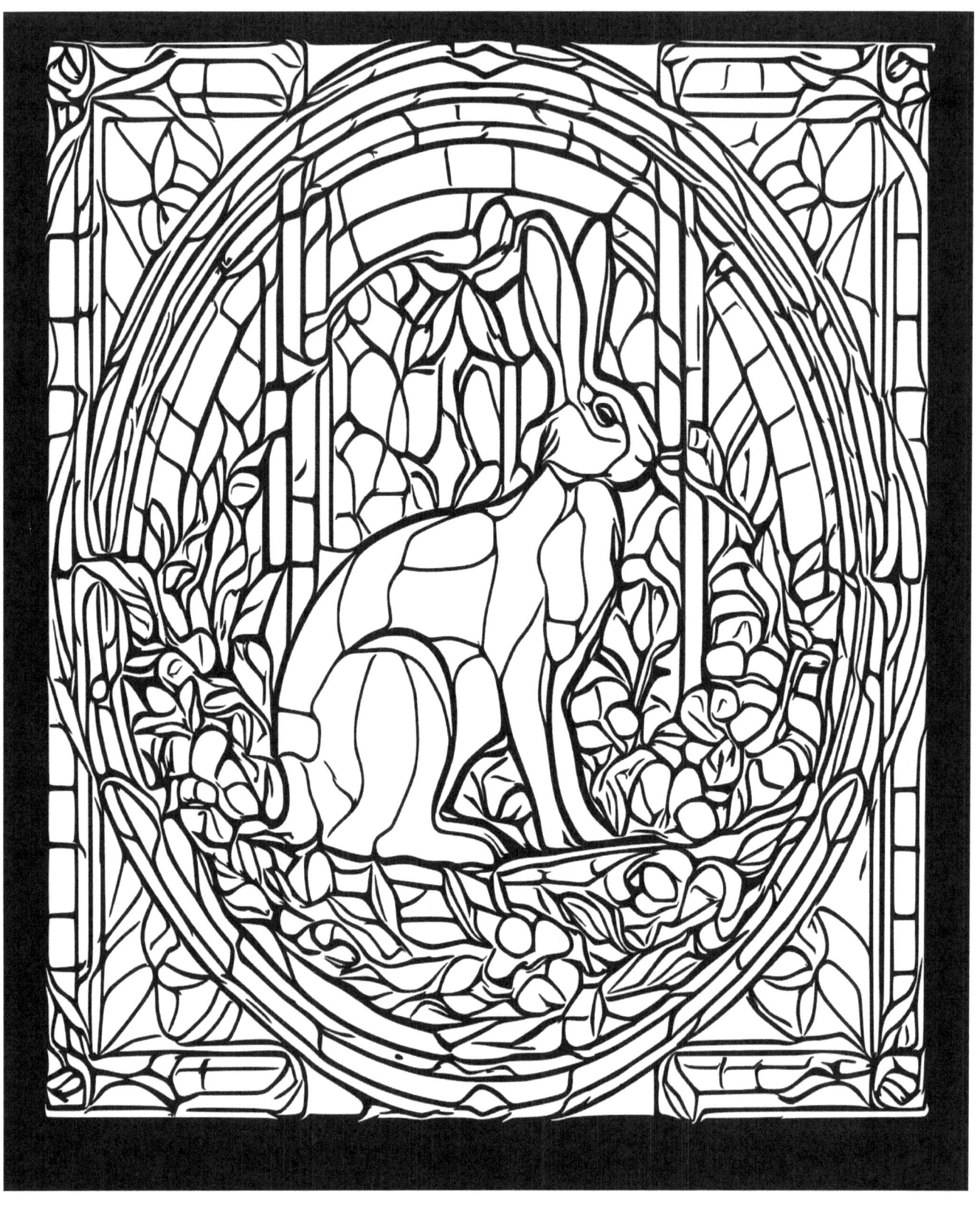

The Easter Bunny

April

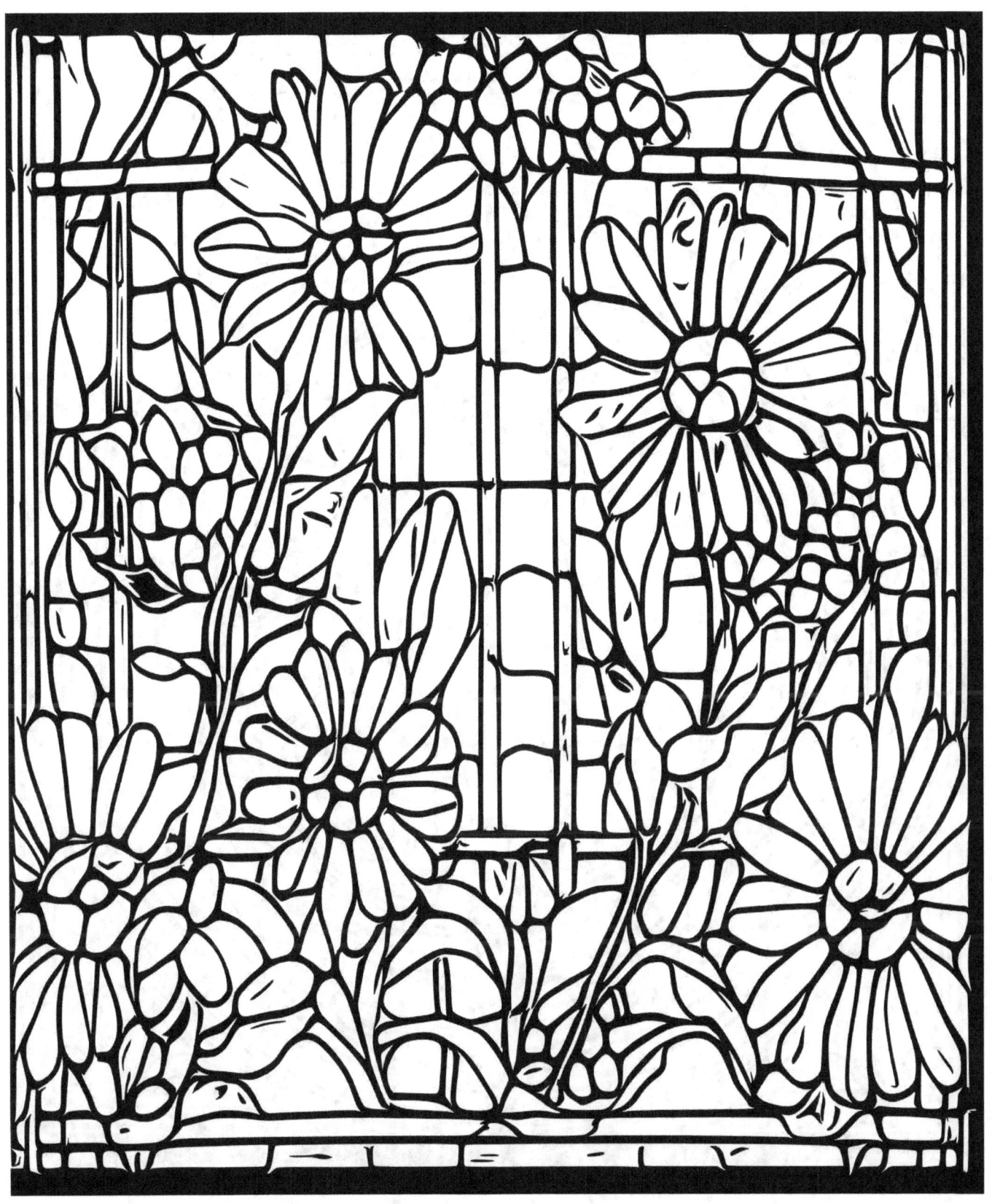

Flower of the Month: Daisy

May

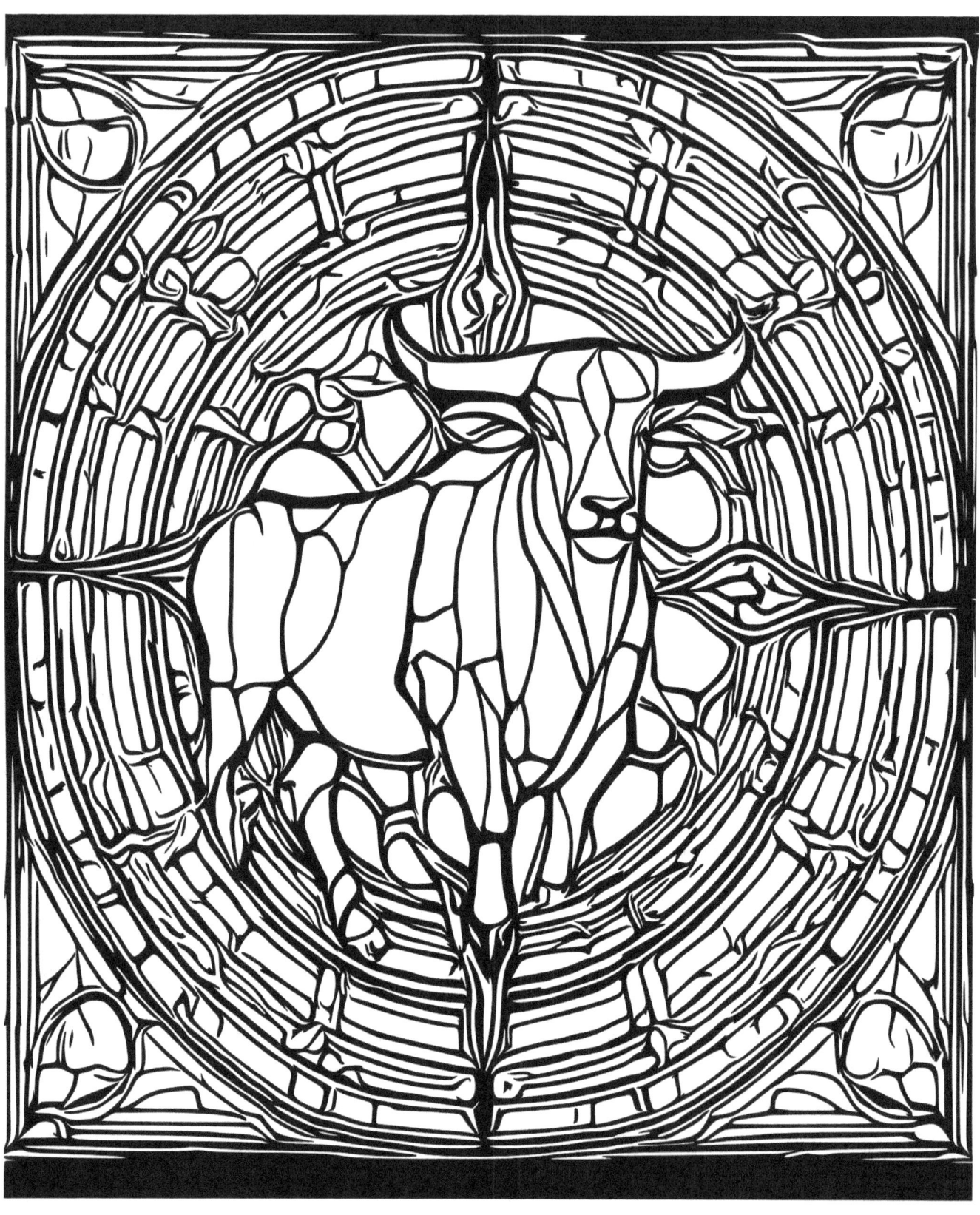

Taurus

May

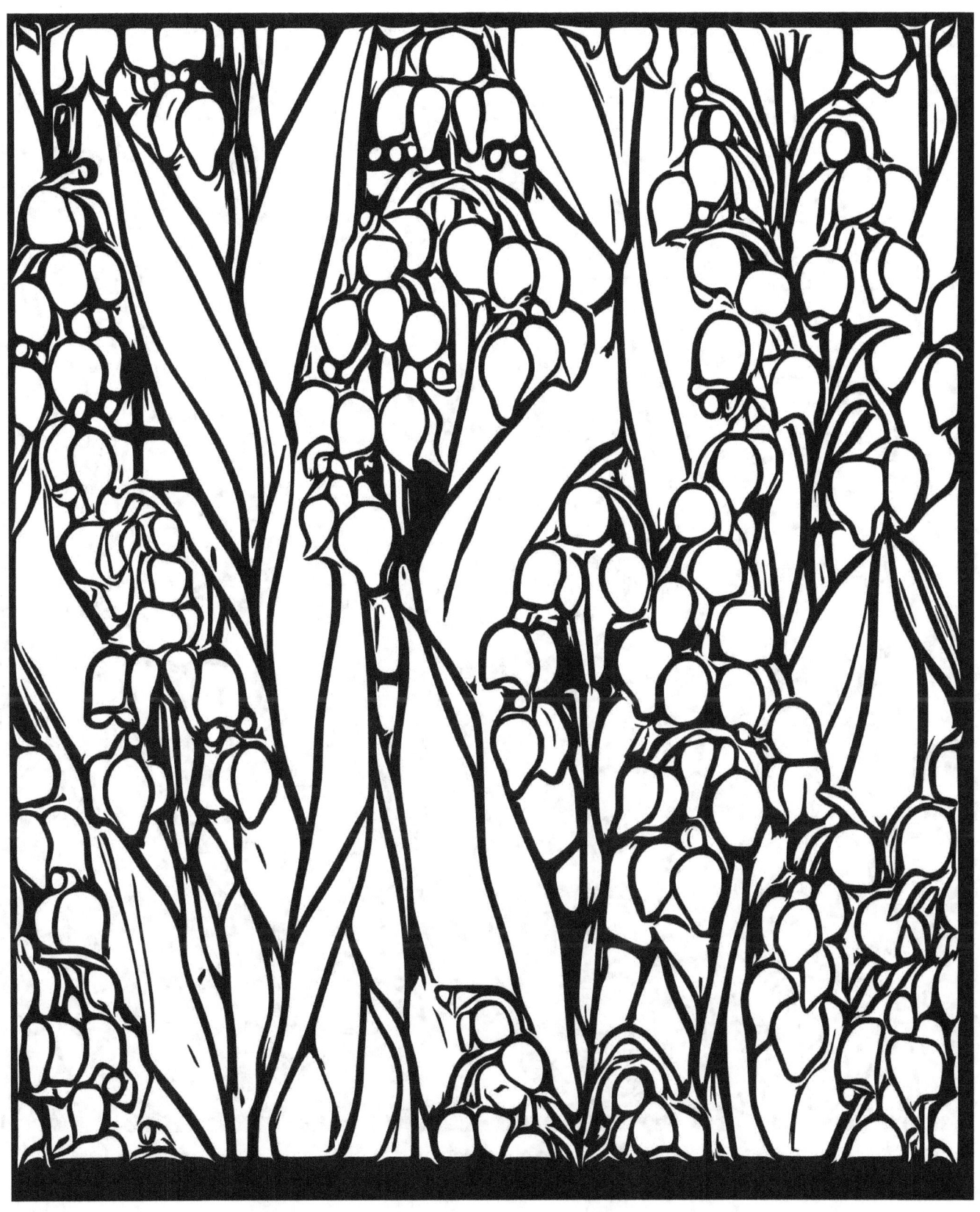

Flower of the Month: Lily of the Valley

May

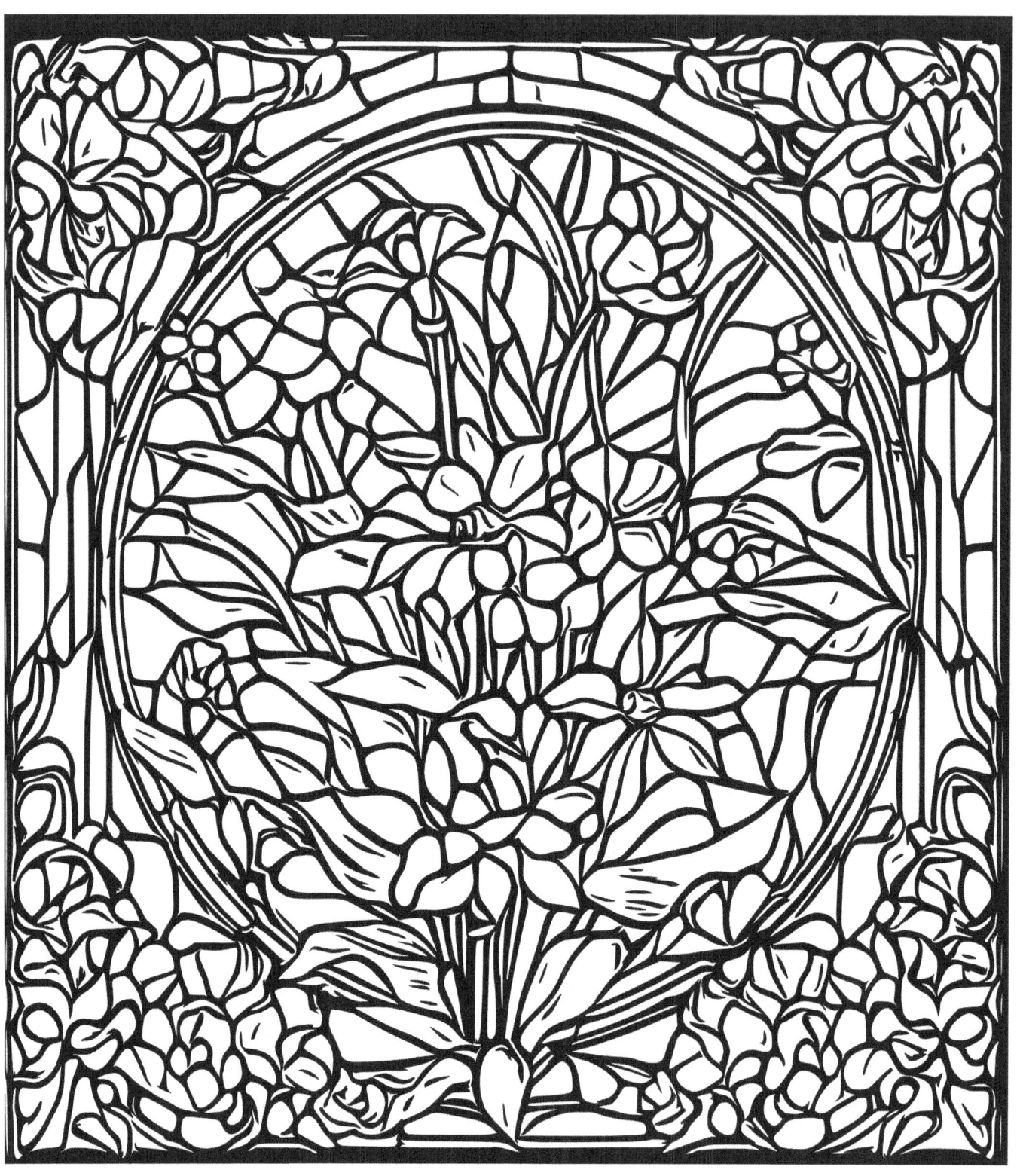

Spring in Full Swing

May

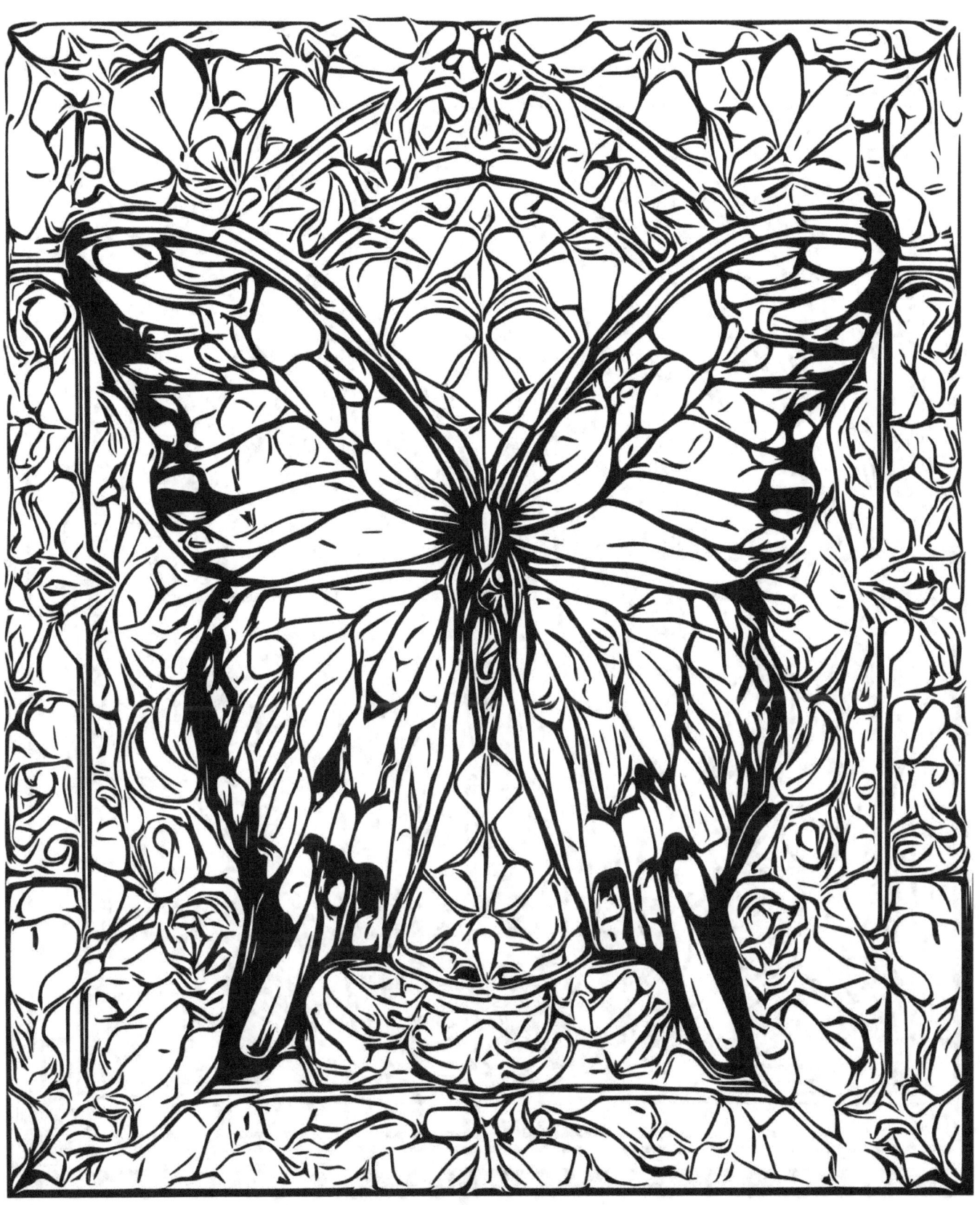

Butterflies Emerge

June

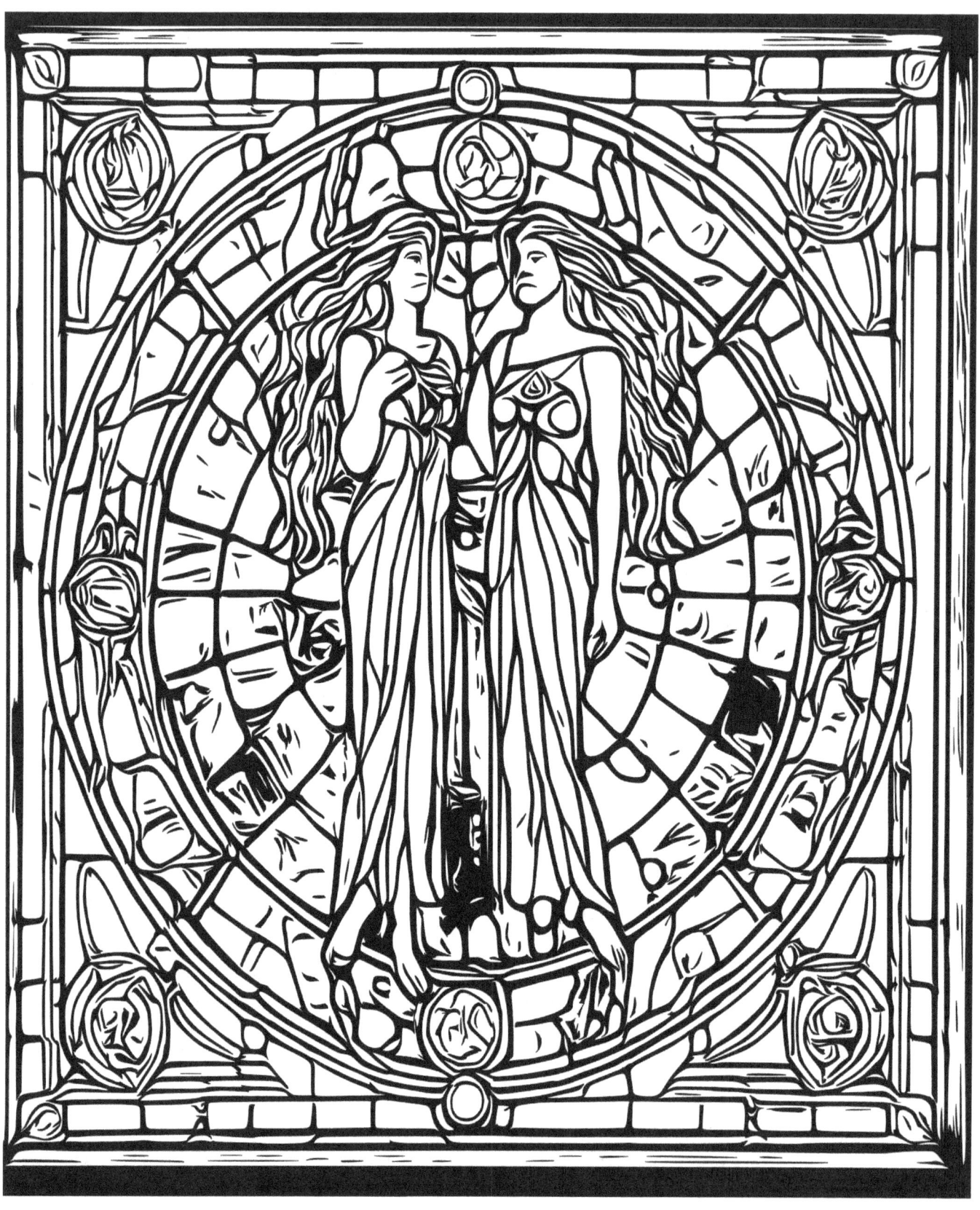

Gemini

June

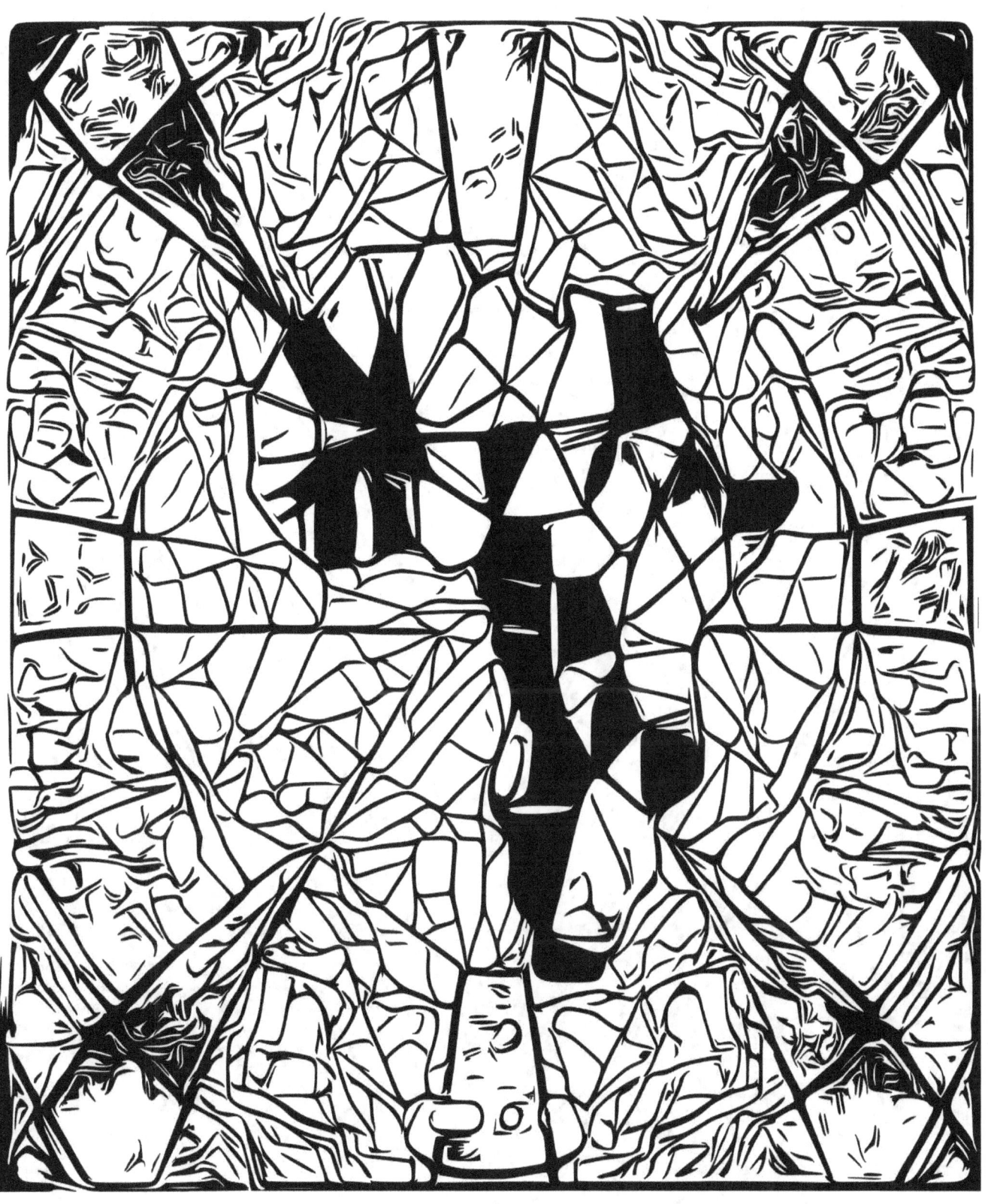

Juneteenth: The Celebration of Freedom Day

June

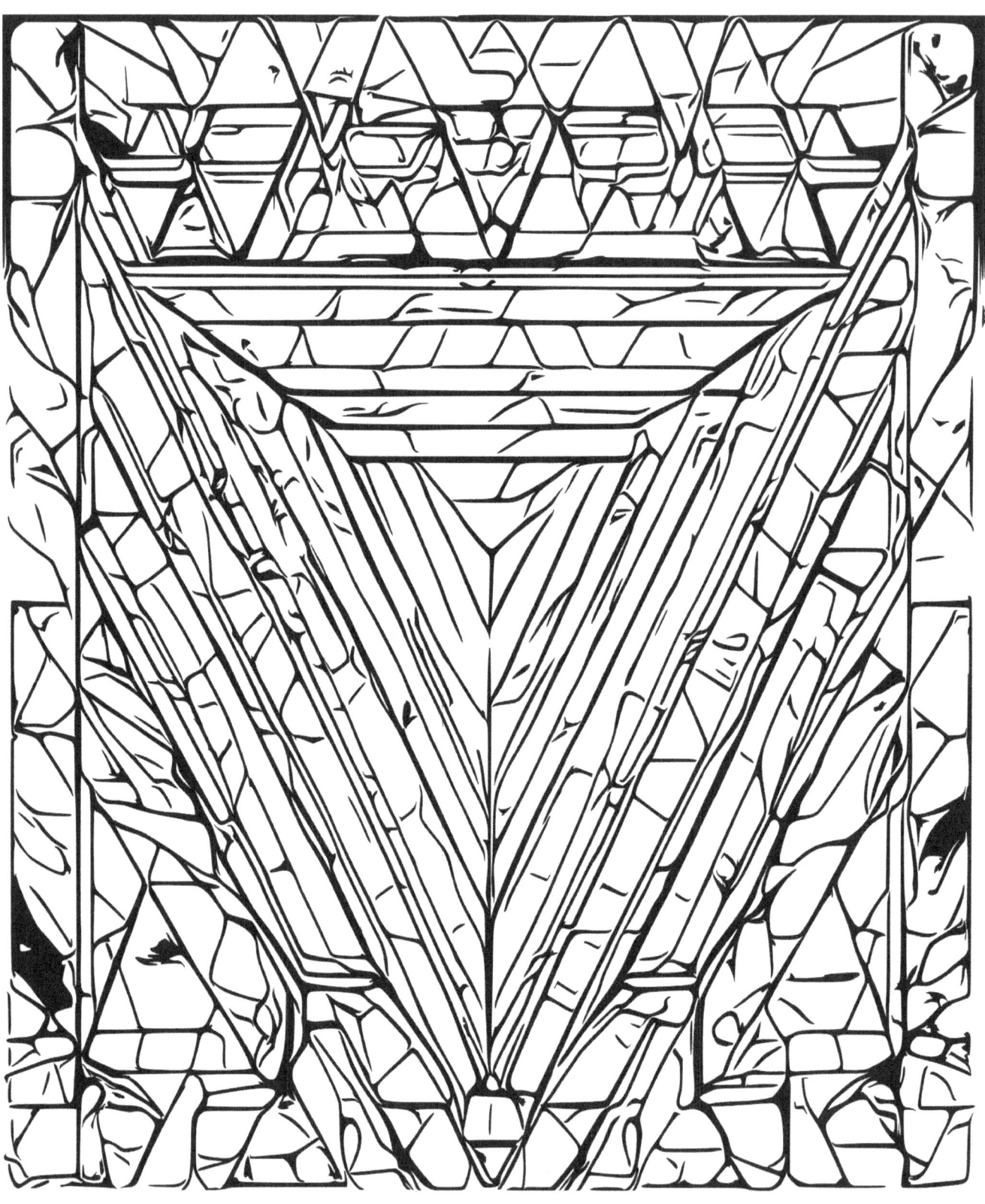

Pride Month Pink Triangle

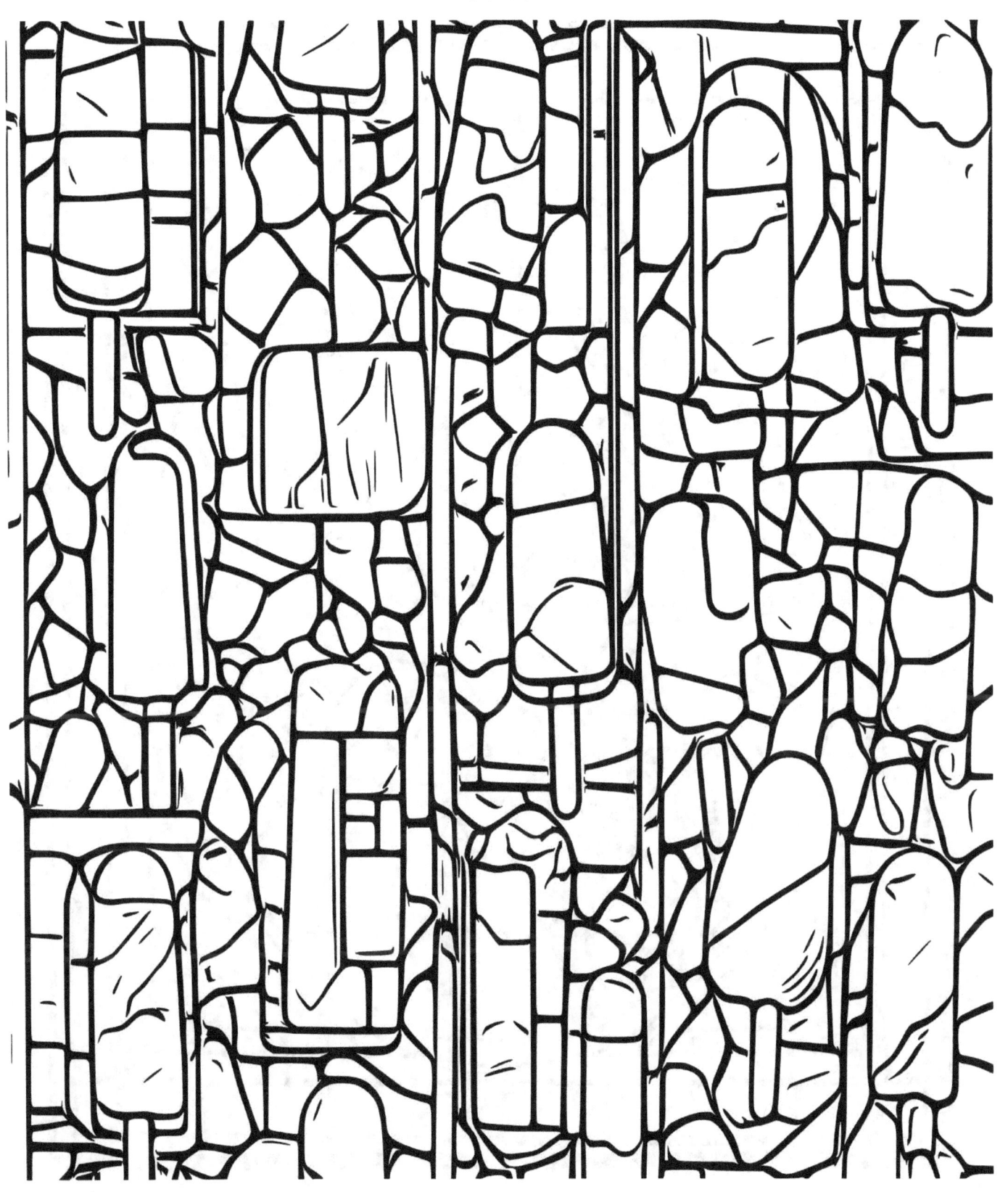

Keepin' Cool Popsicles

June

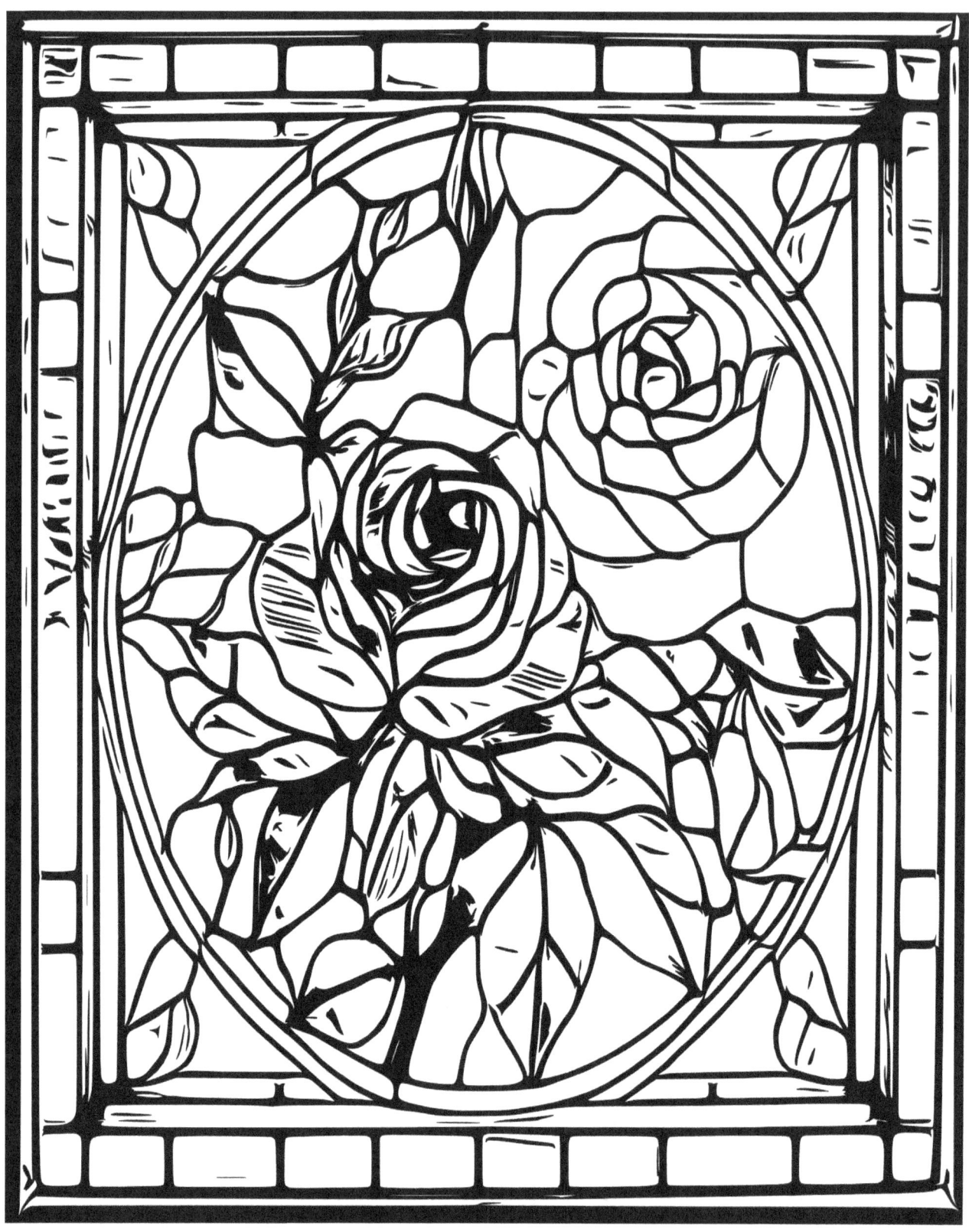

Flower of the Month: Rose

July

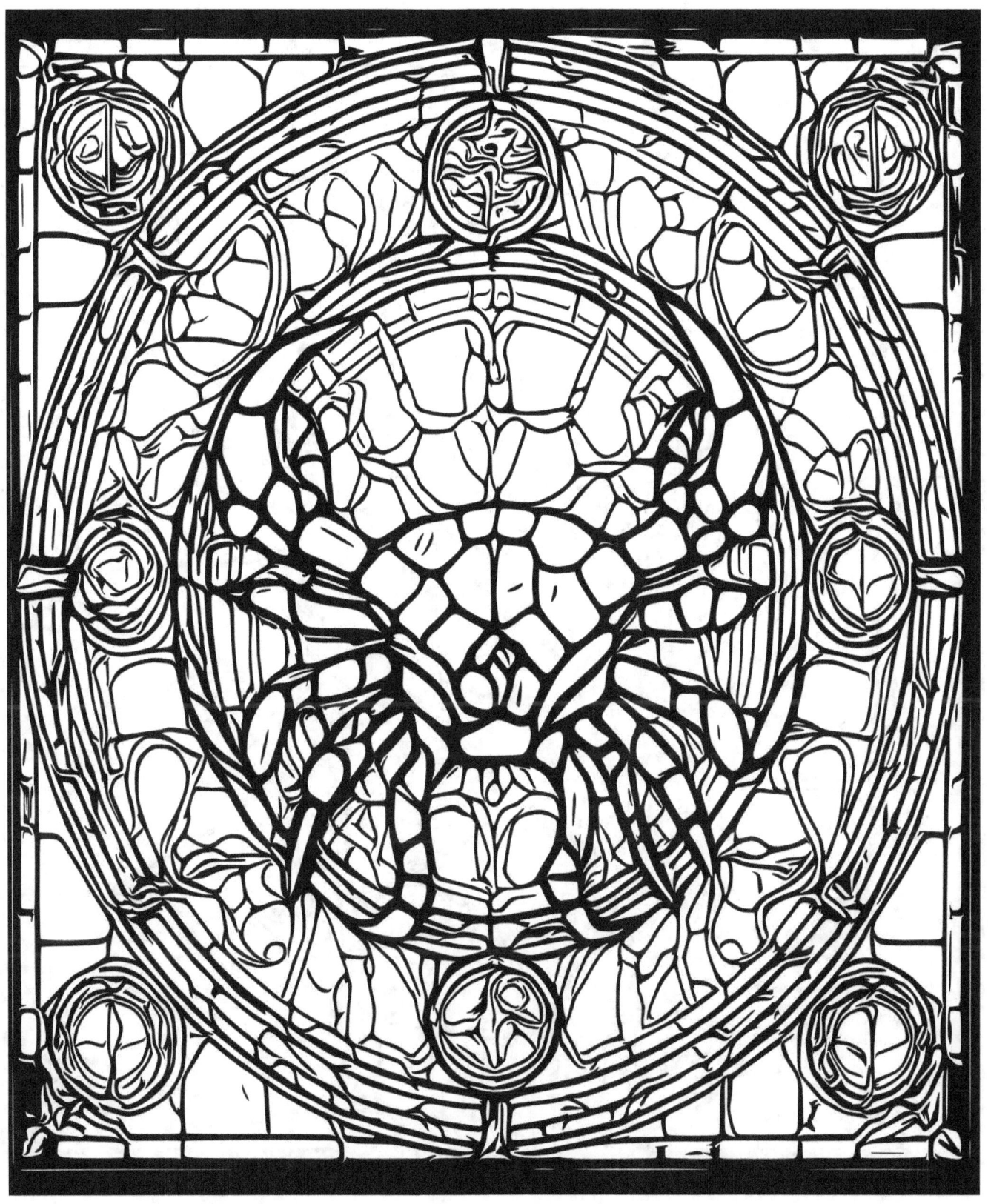

Cancer

July

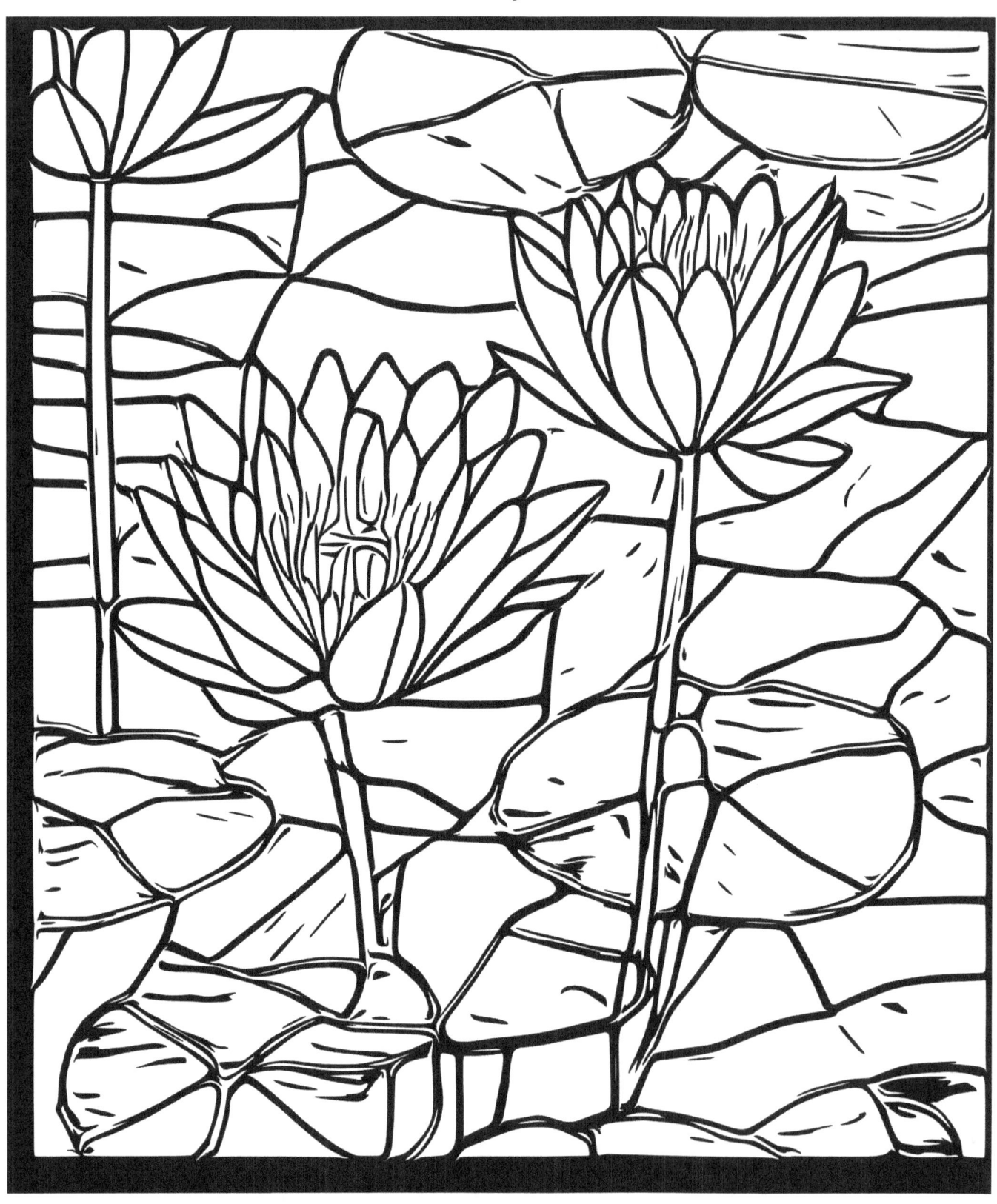

Flower of the Month: Water Lily

July

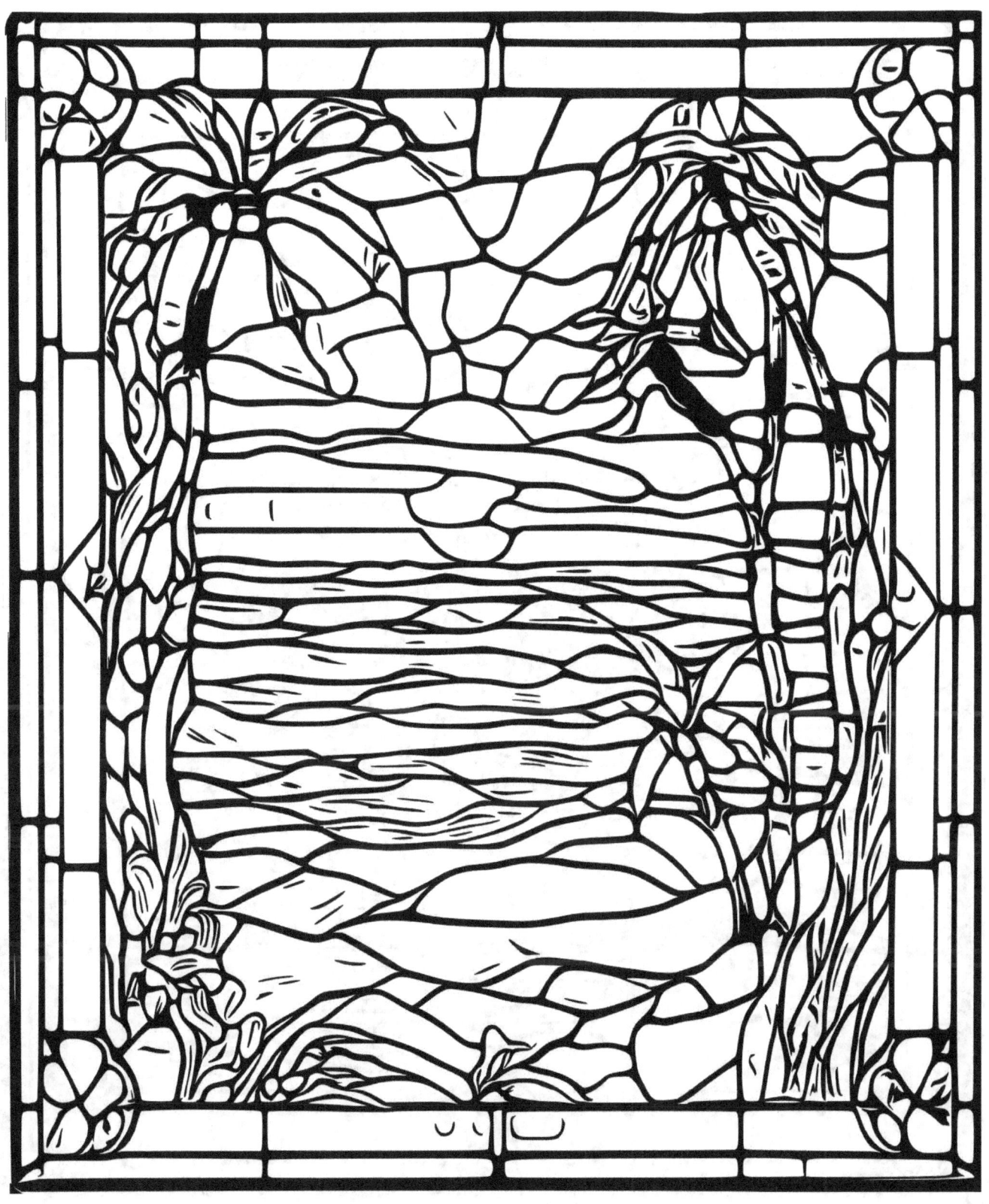

Sunset at the Beach

July

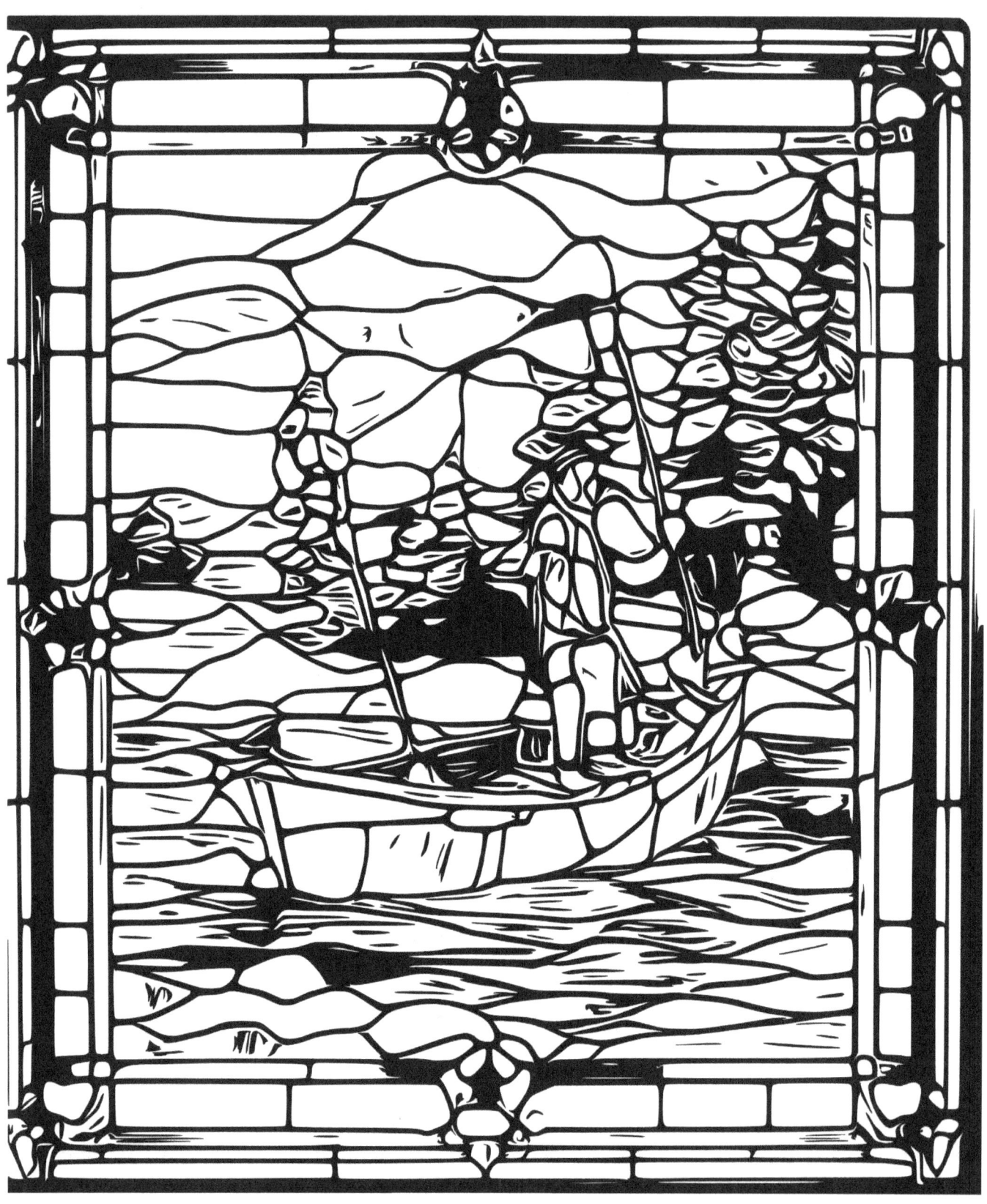

Gone Fishin'

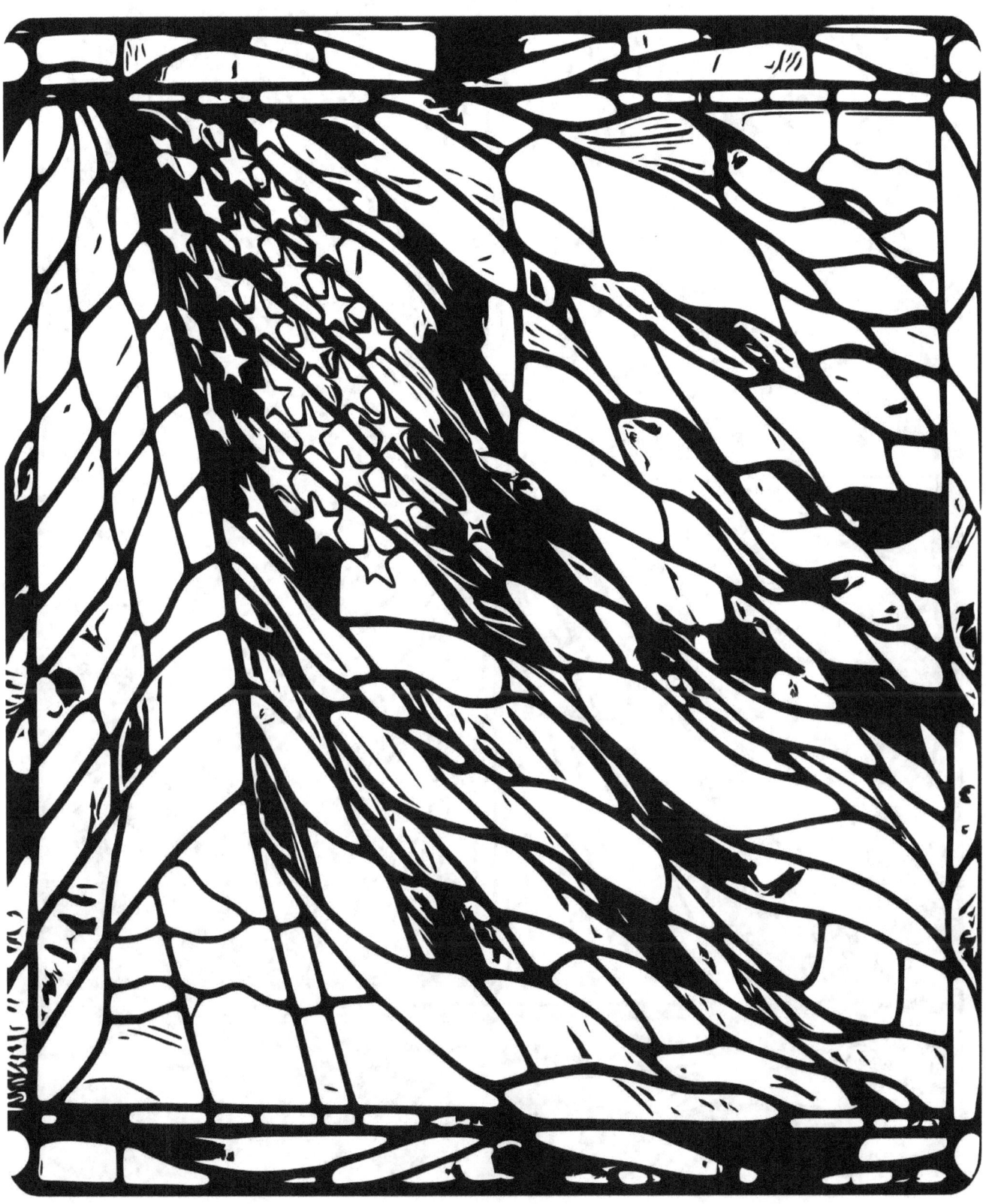

American Flag

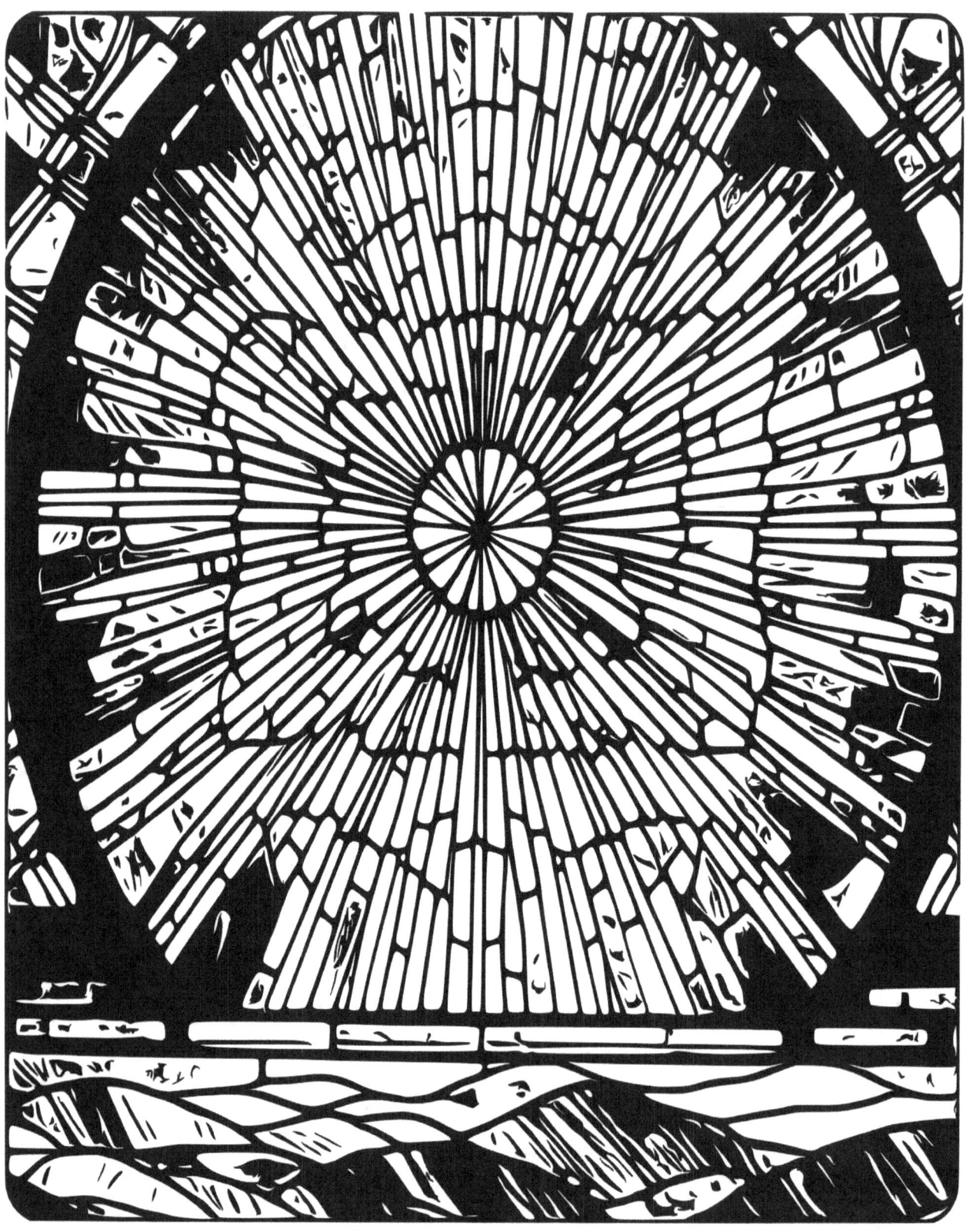

Fireworks

July

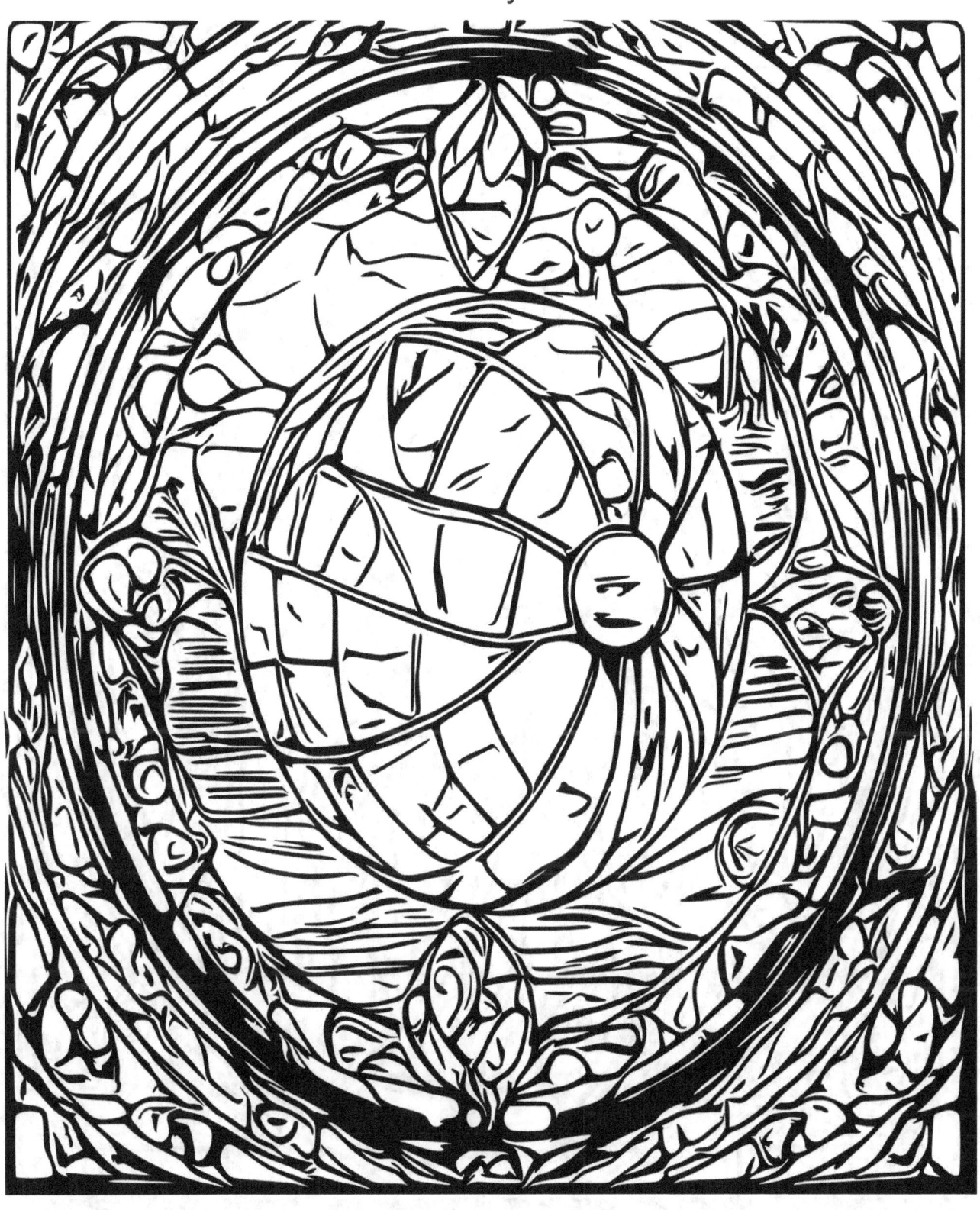

Beach Ball

August

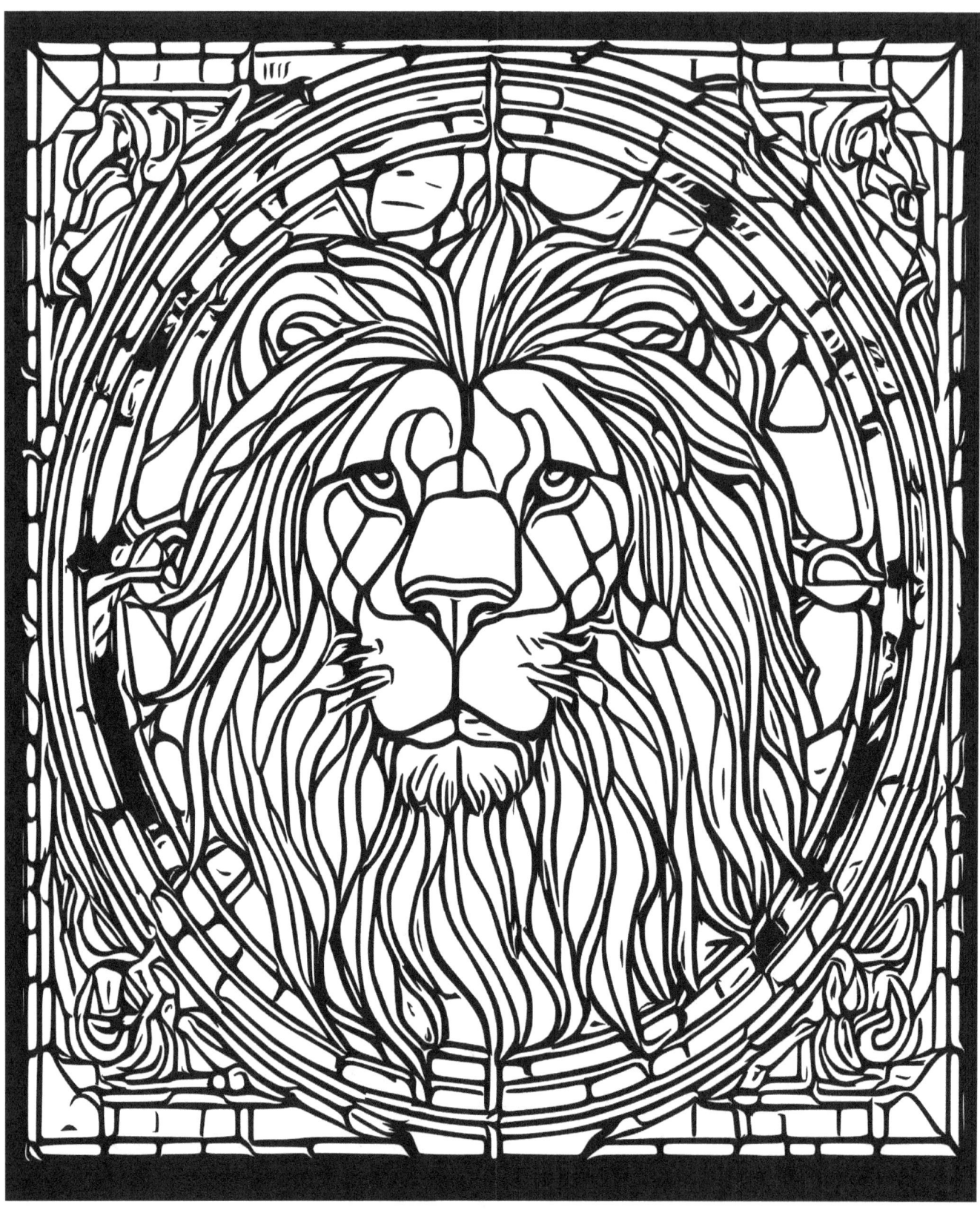

Leo

August

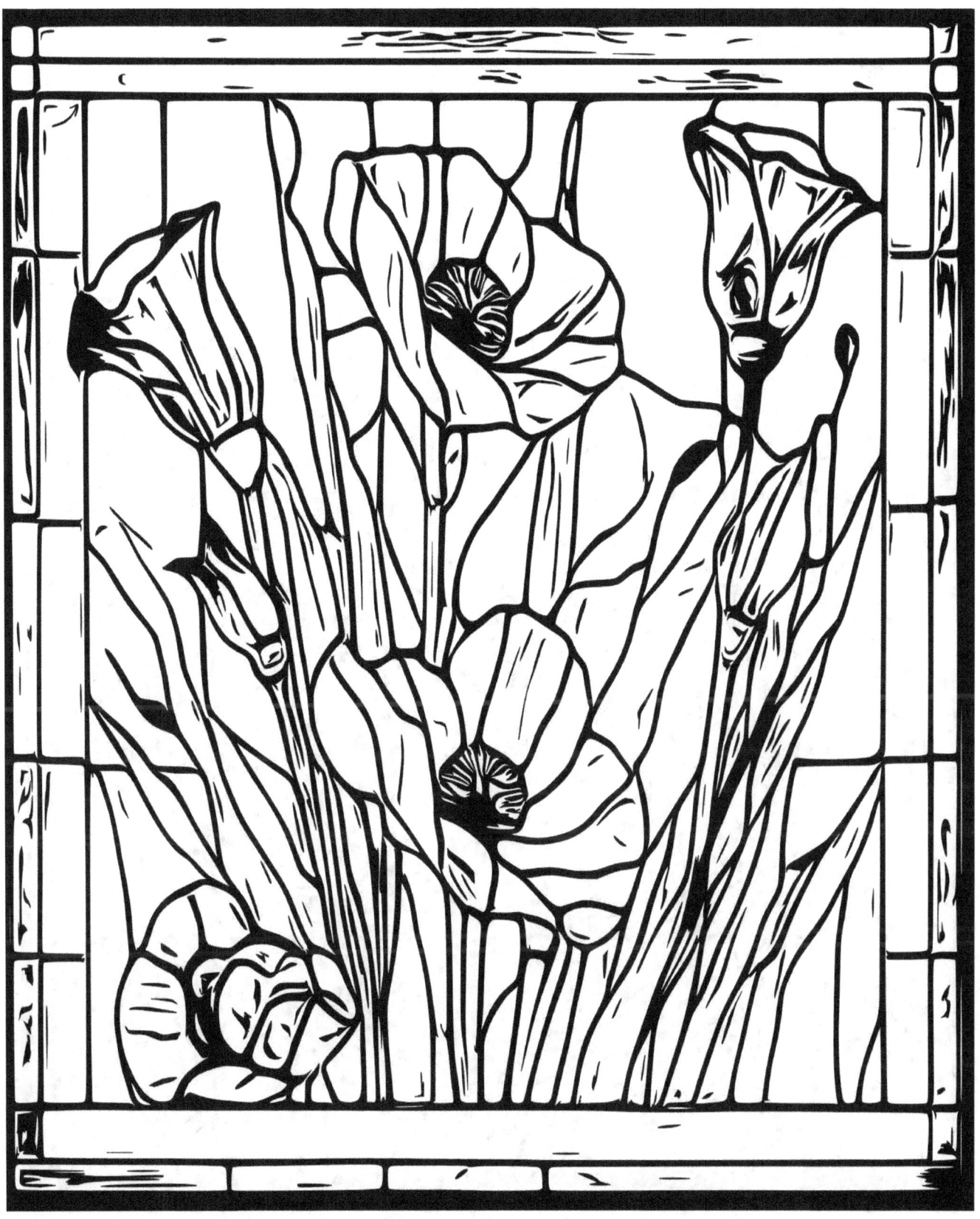

Flower of the Month: Poppy

August

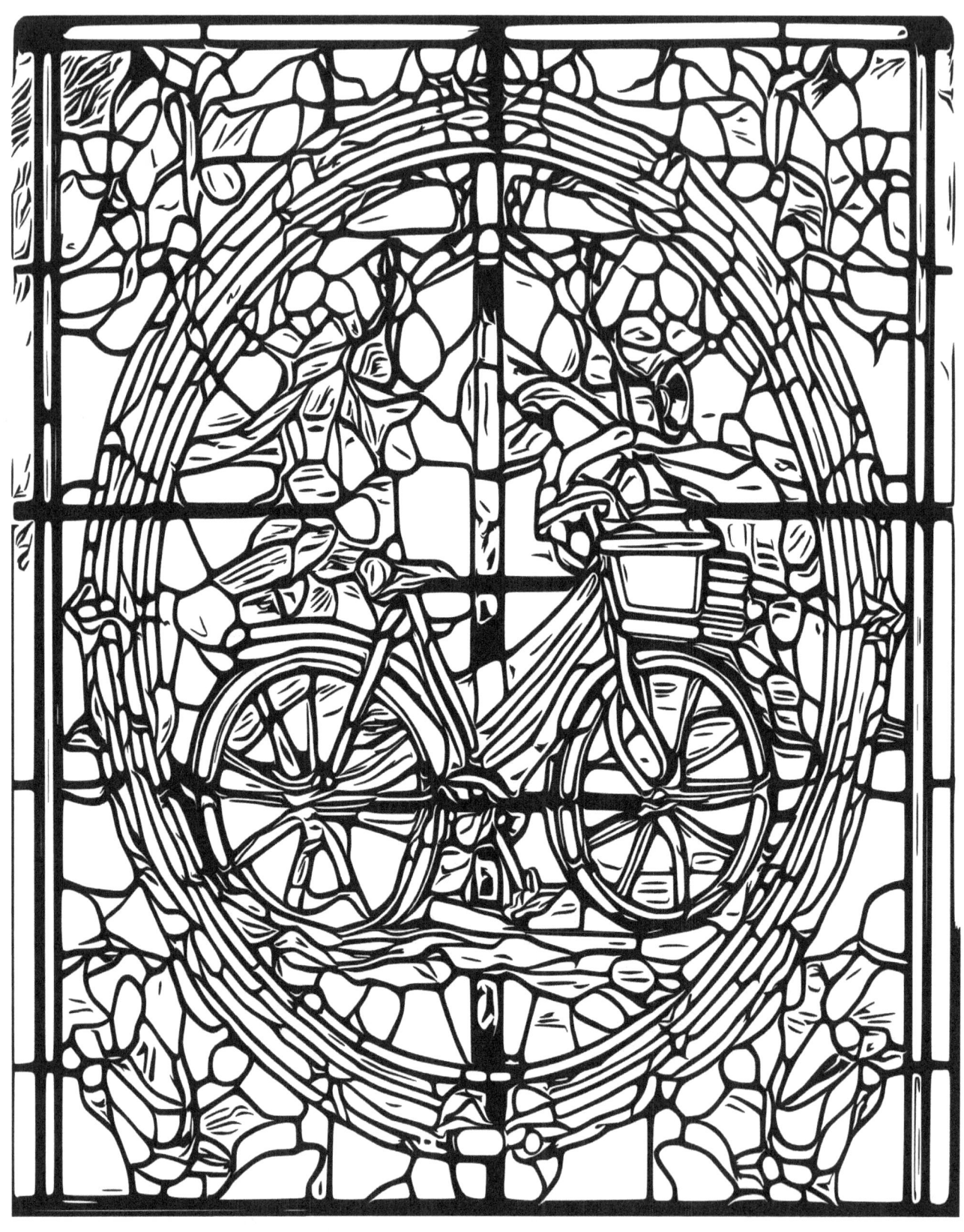

Bike Ride in Nature

August

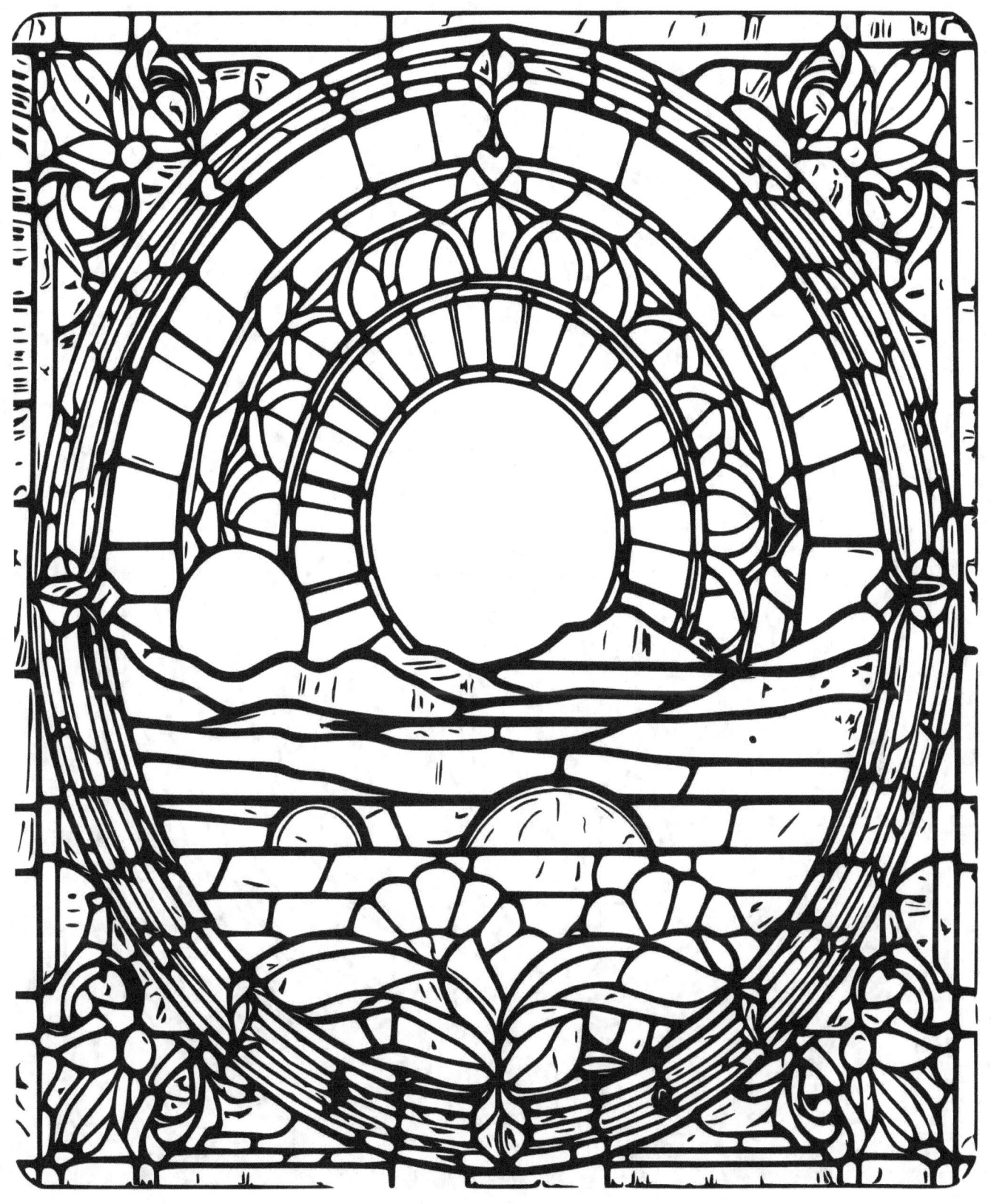

Summer Sunshine

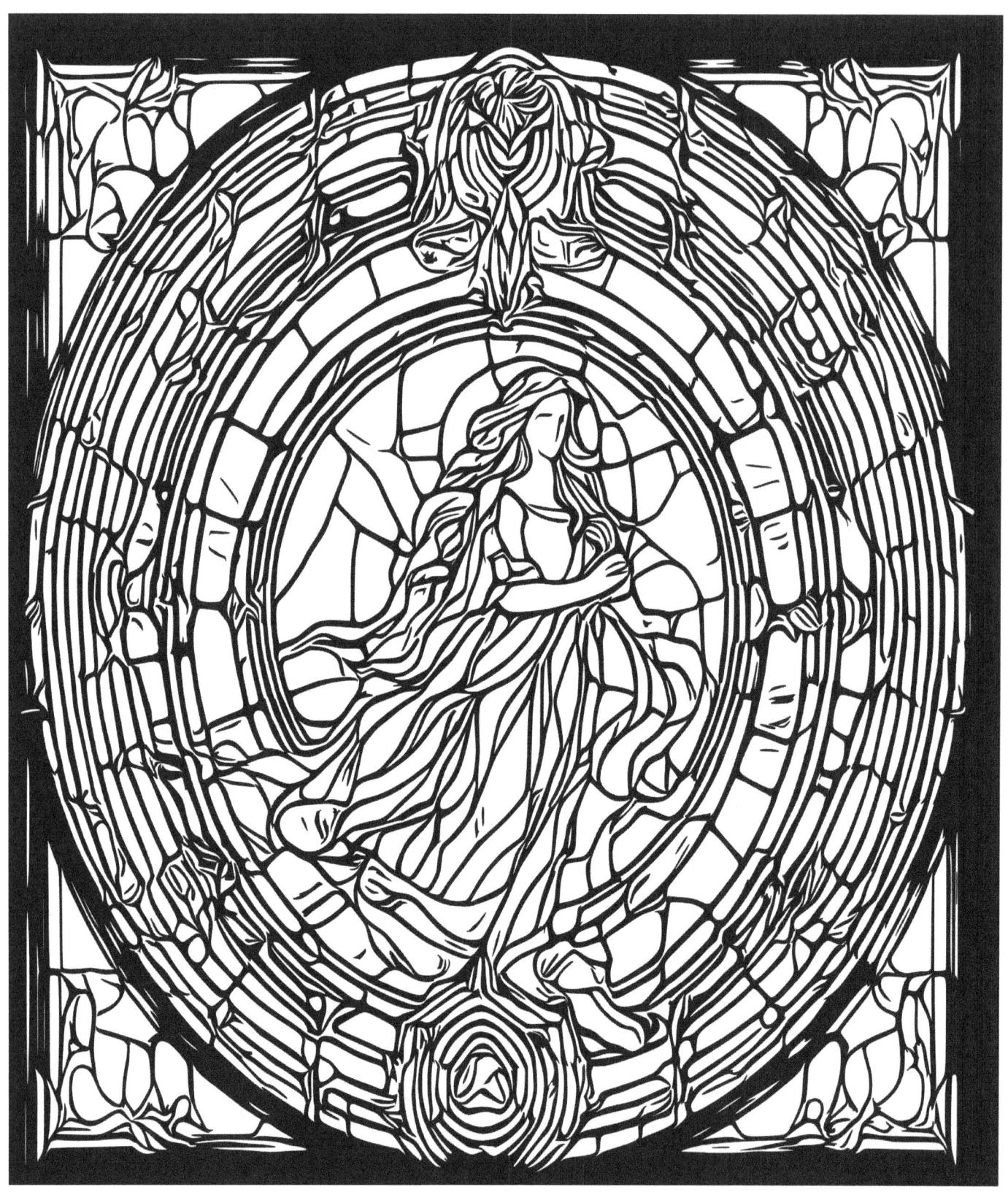

Virgo

September

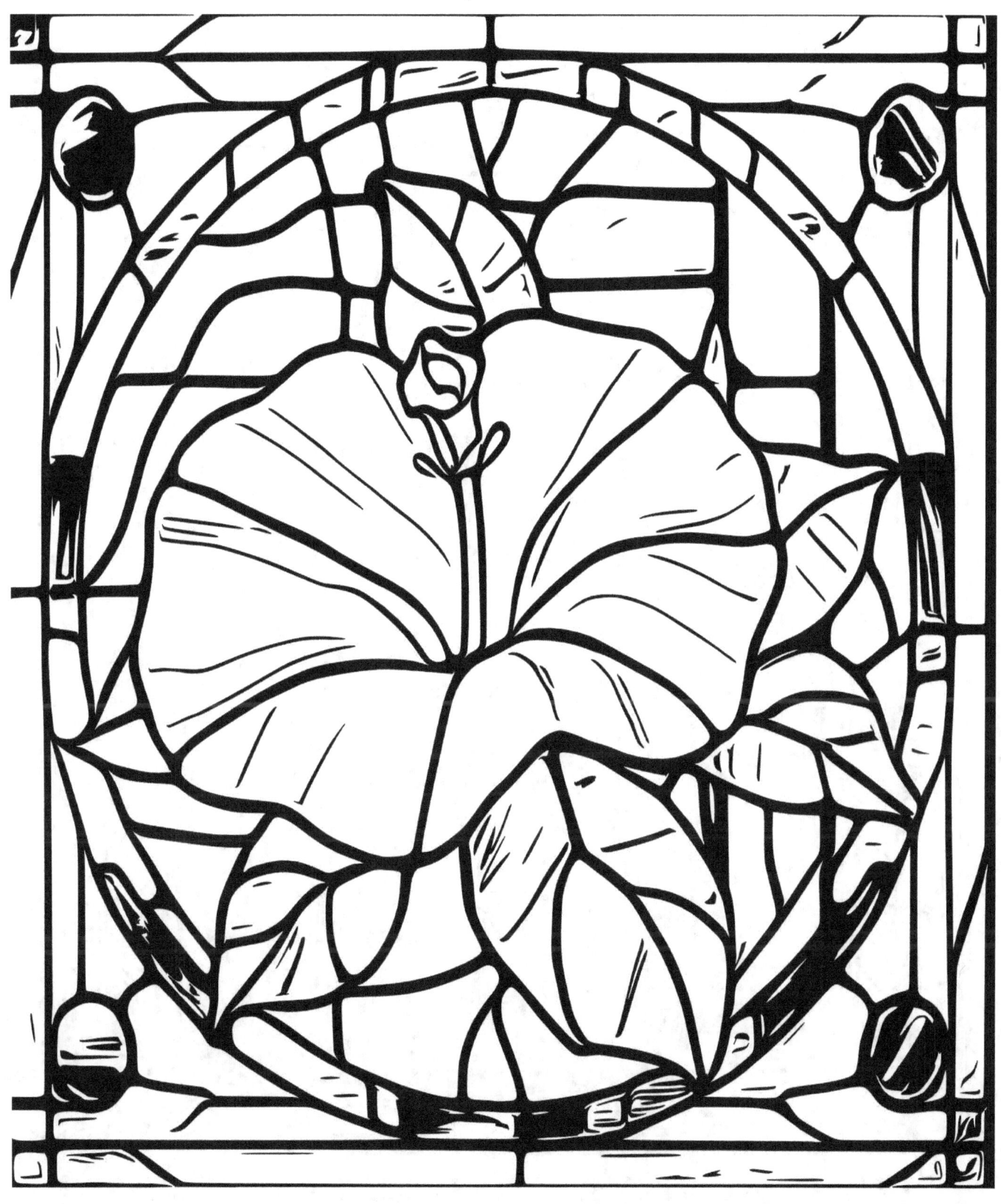

Flower of the Month: Morning Glory

September

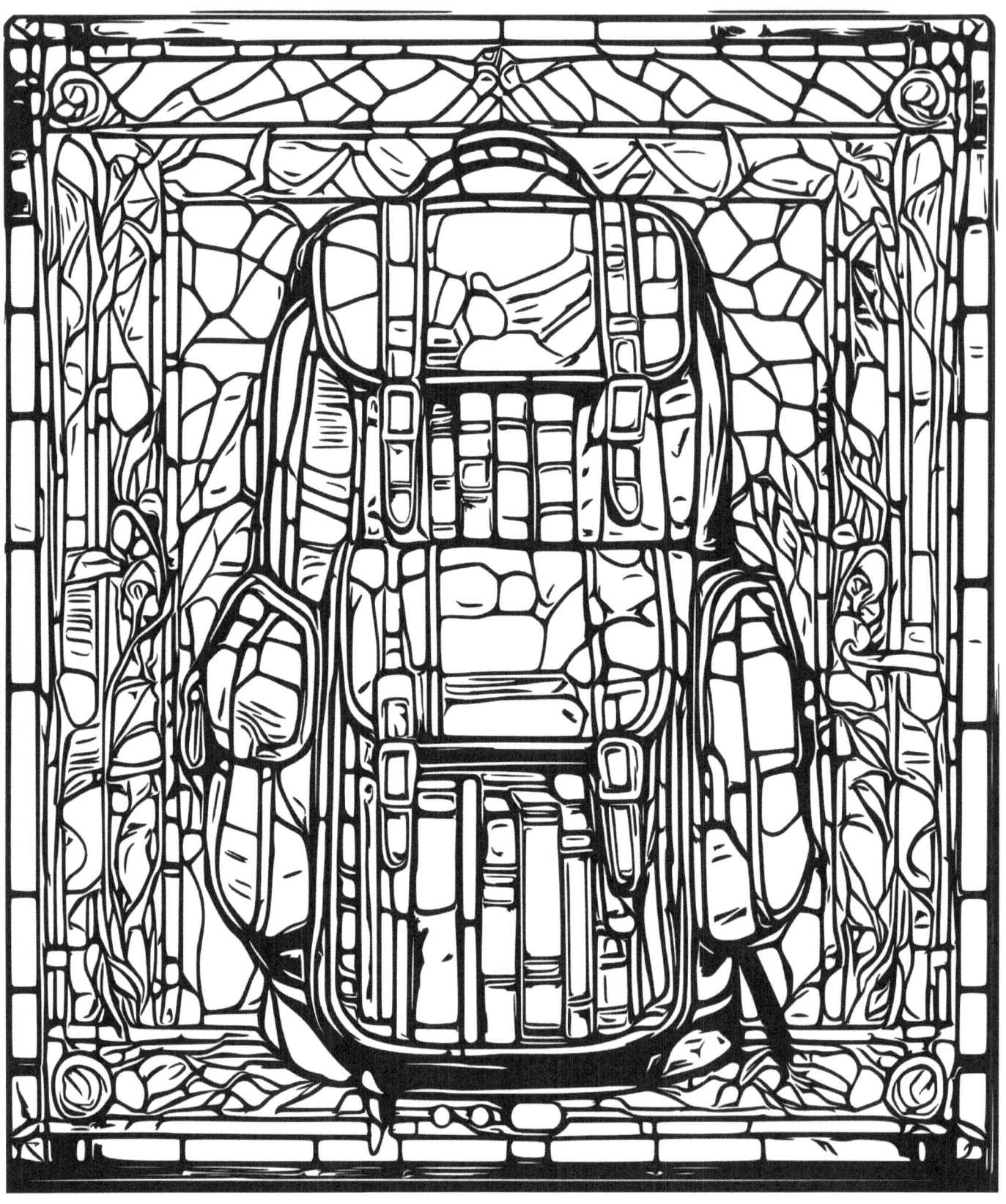

Back to School

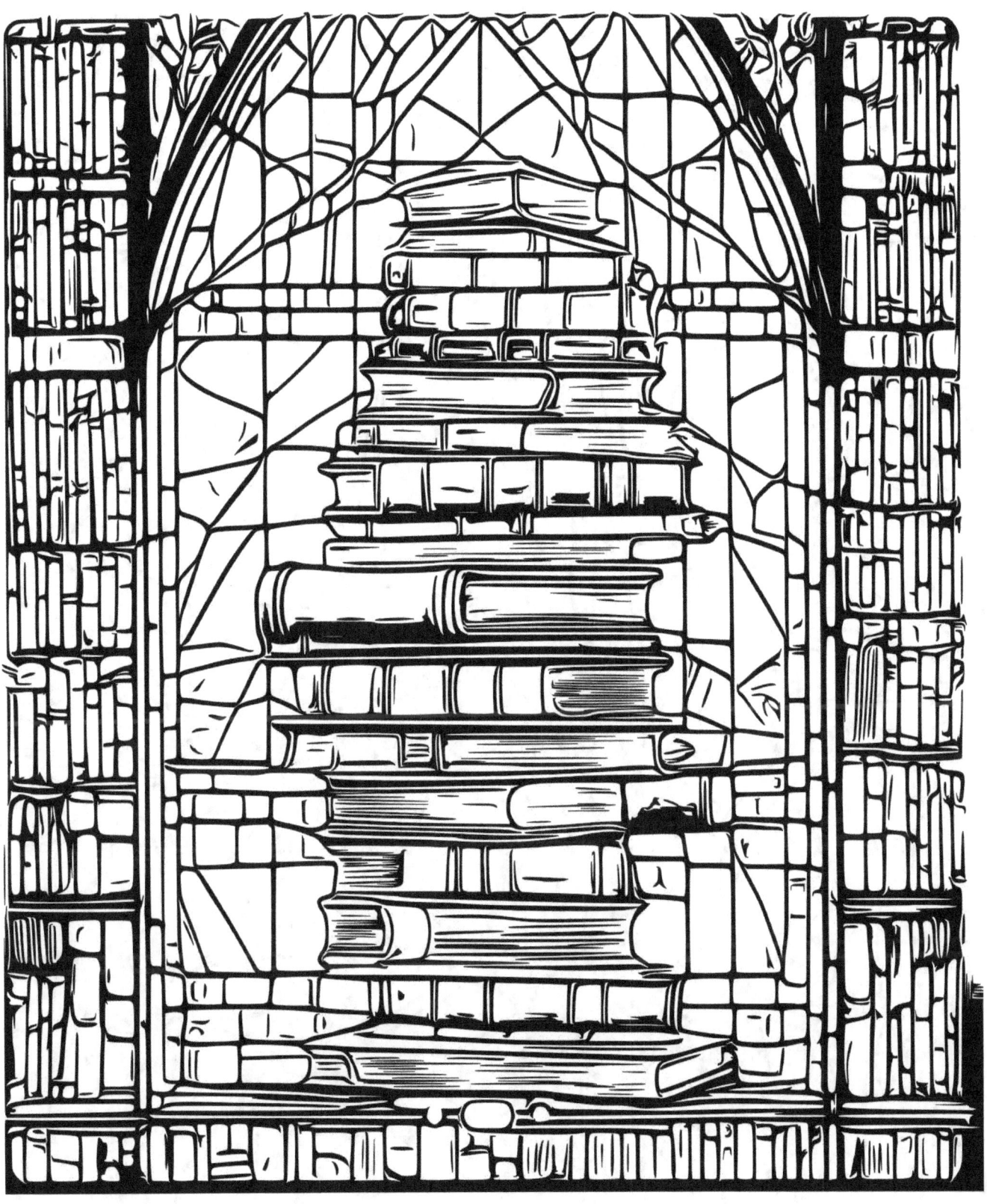

Time to Study Up

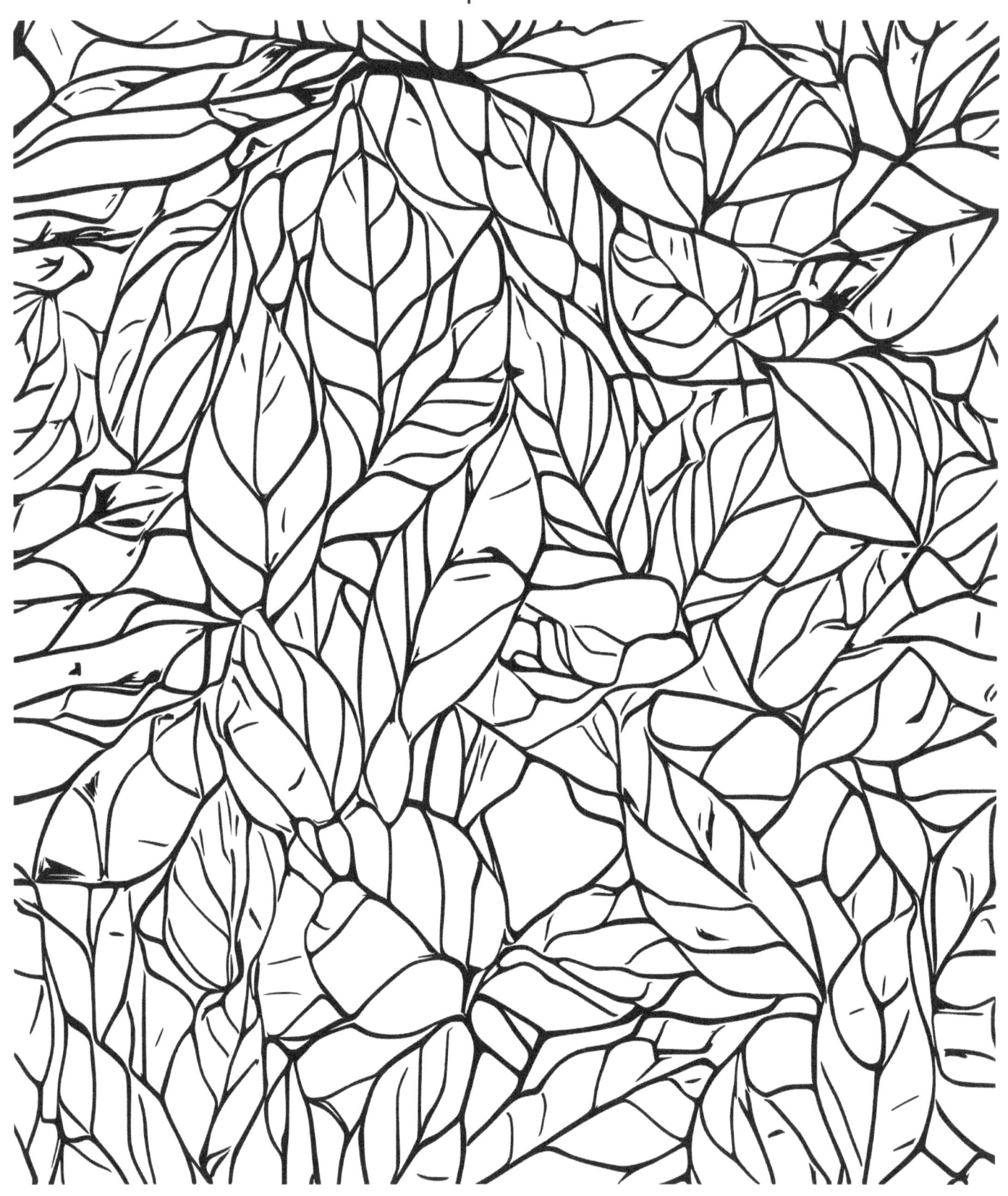

Hello Fall

October

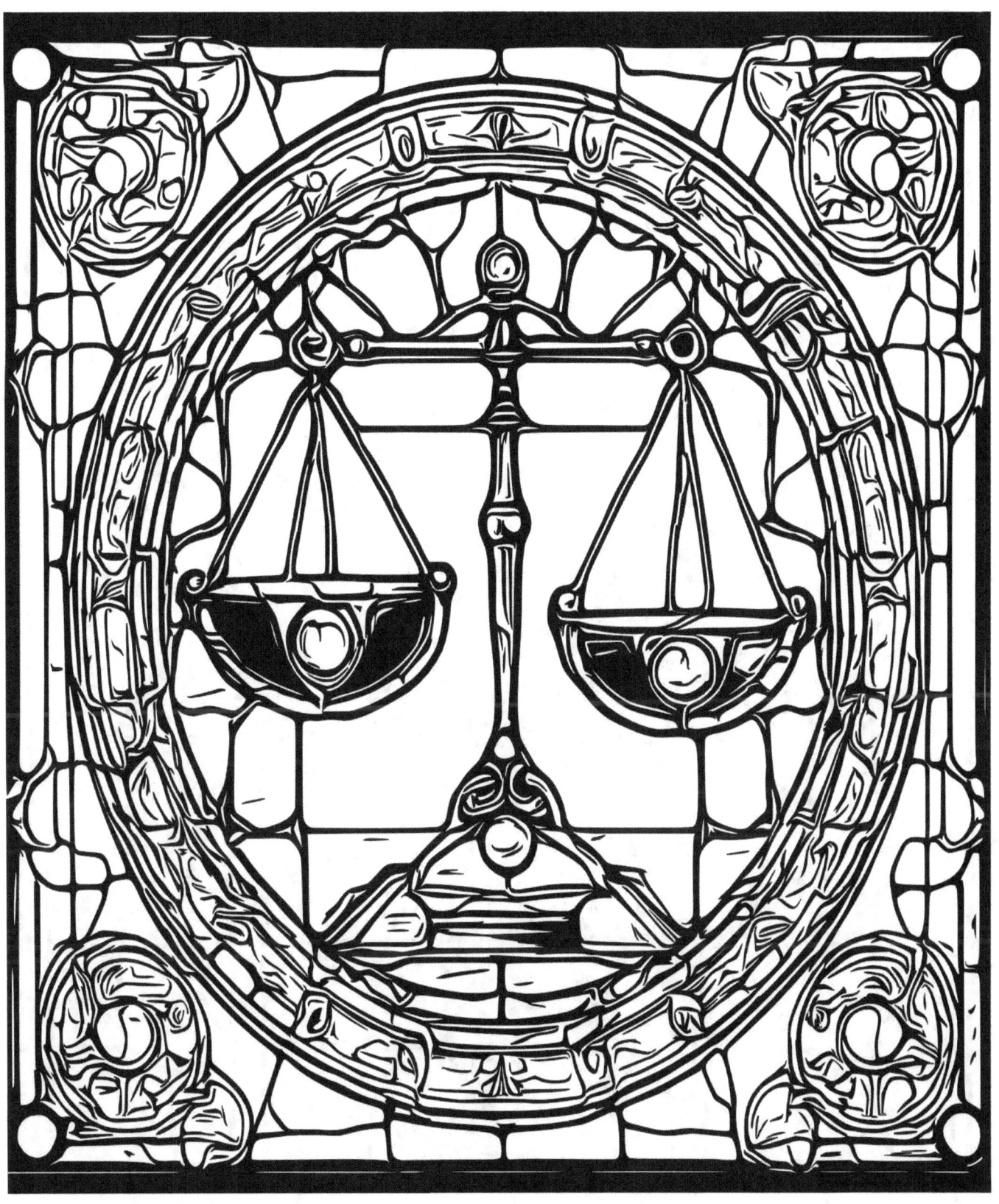

Libra

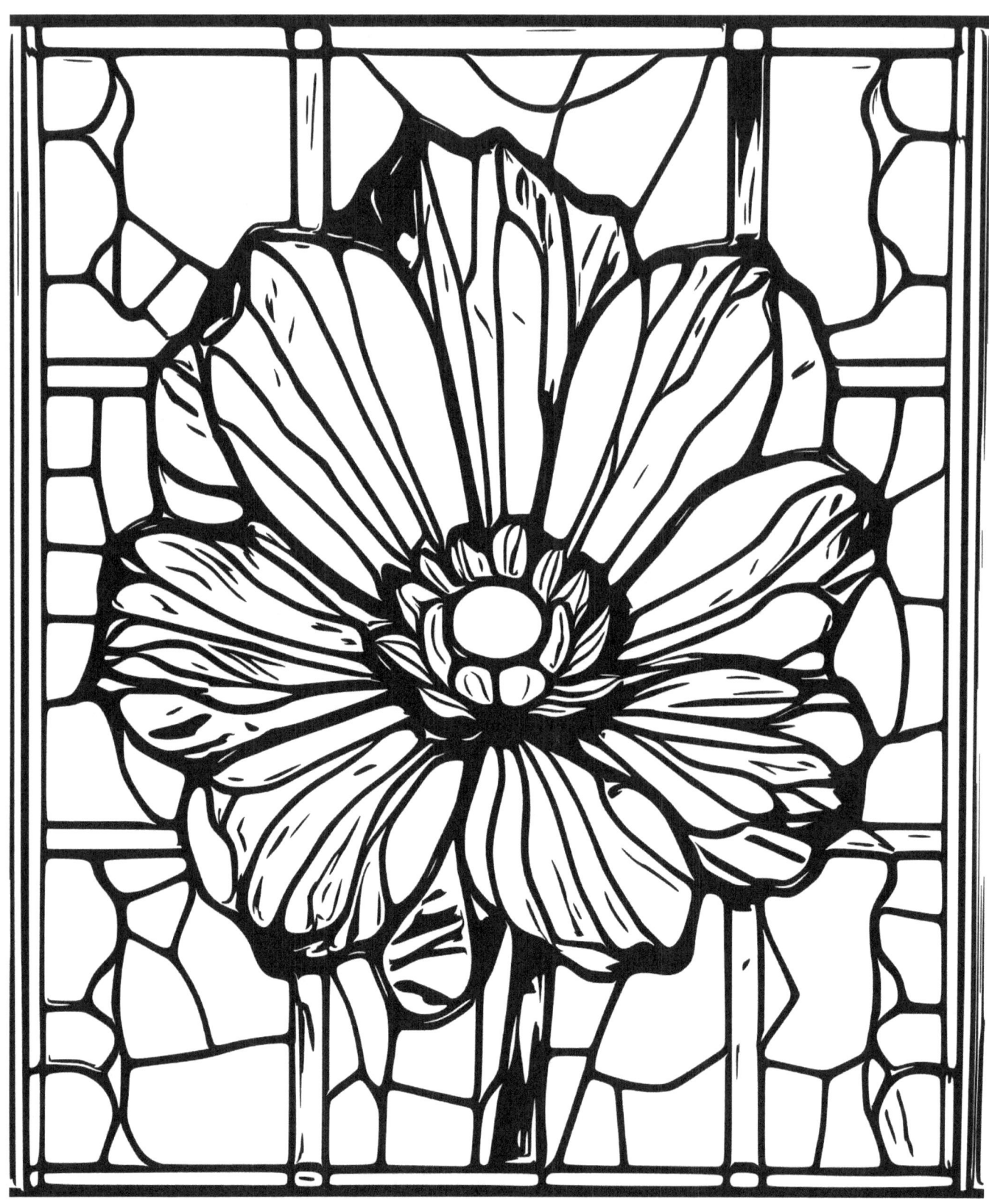

Flower of the Month: Cosmos

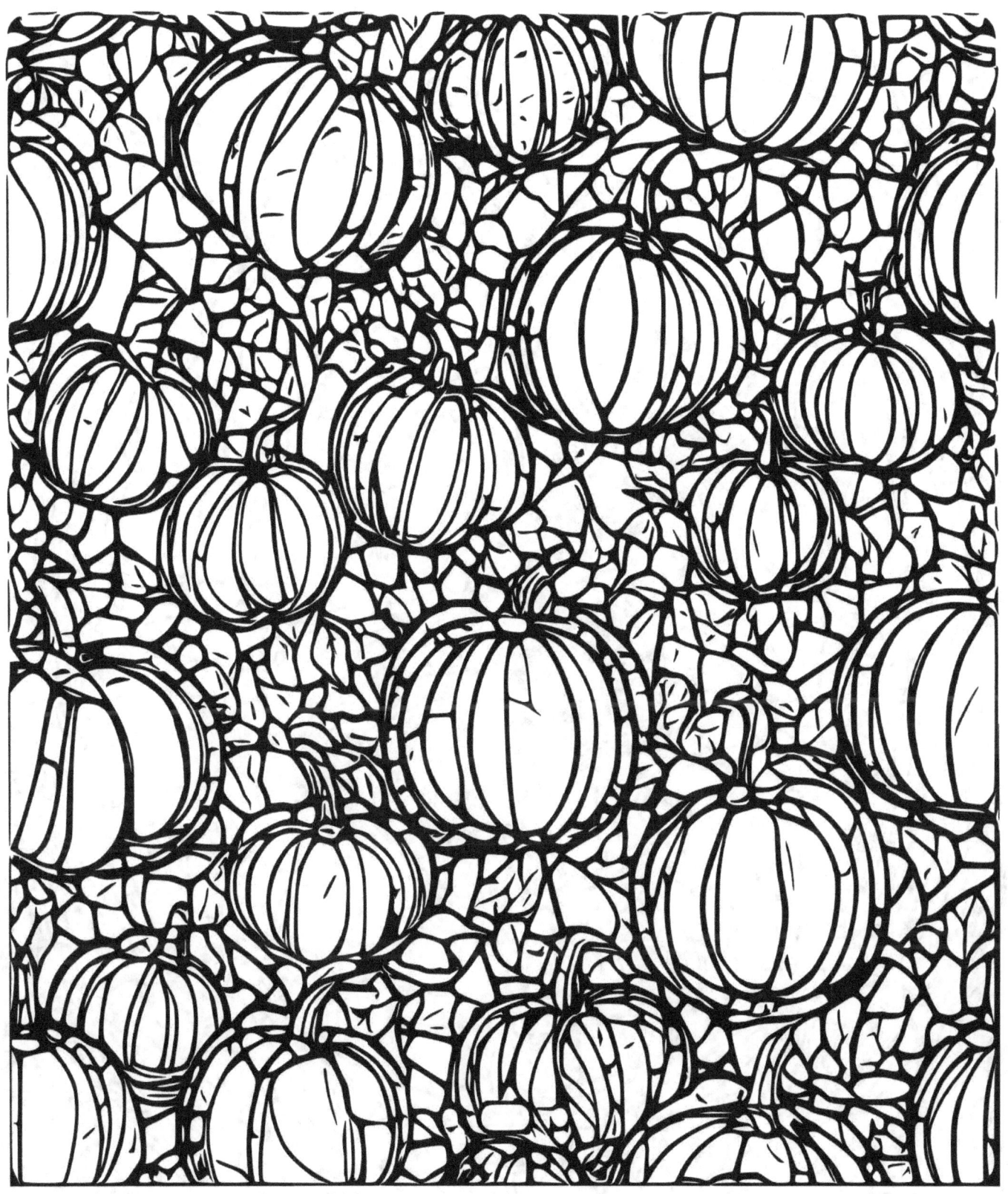

Pumpkin Patchin' Time

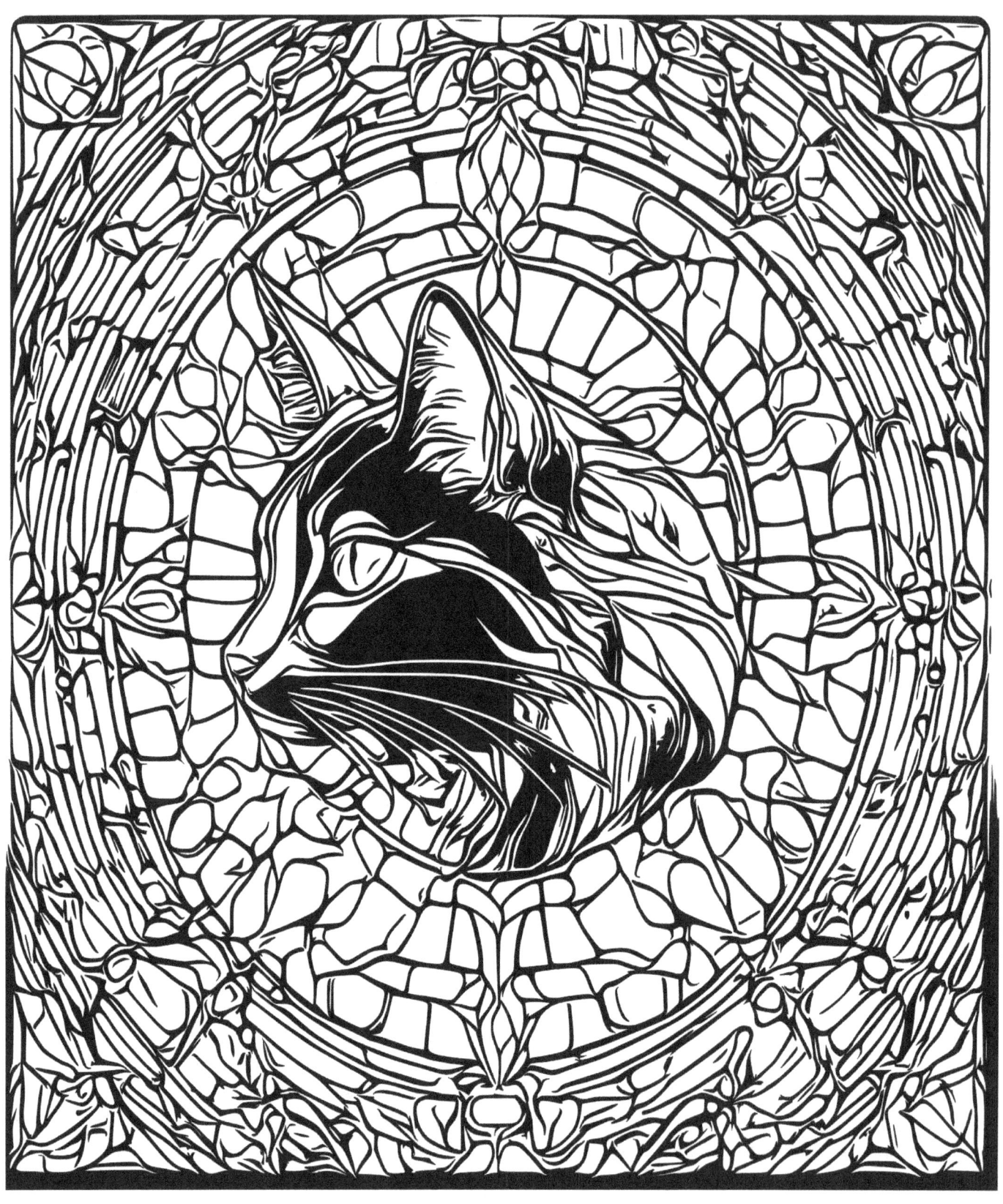

Black Cat 1

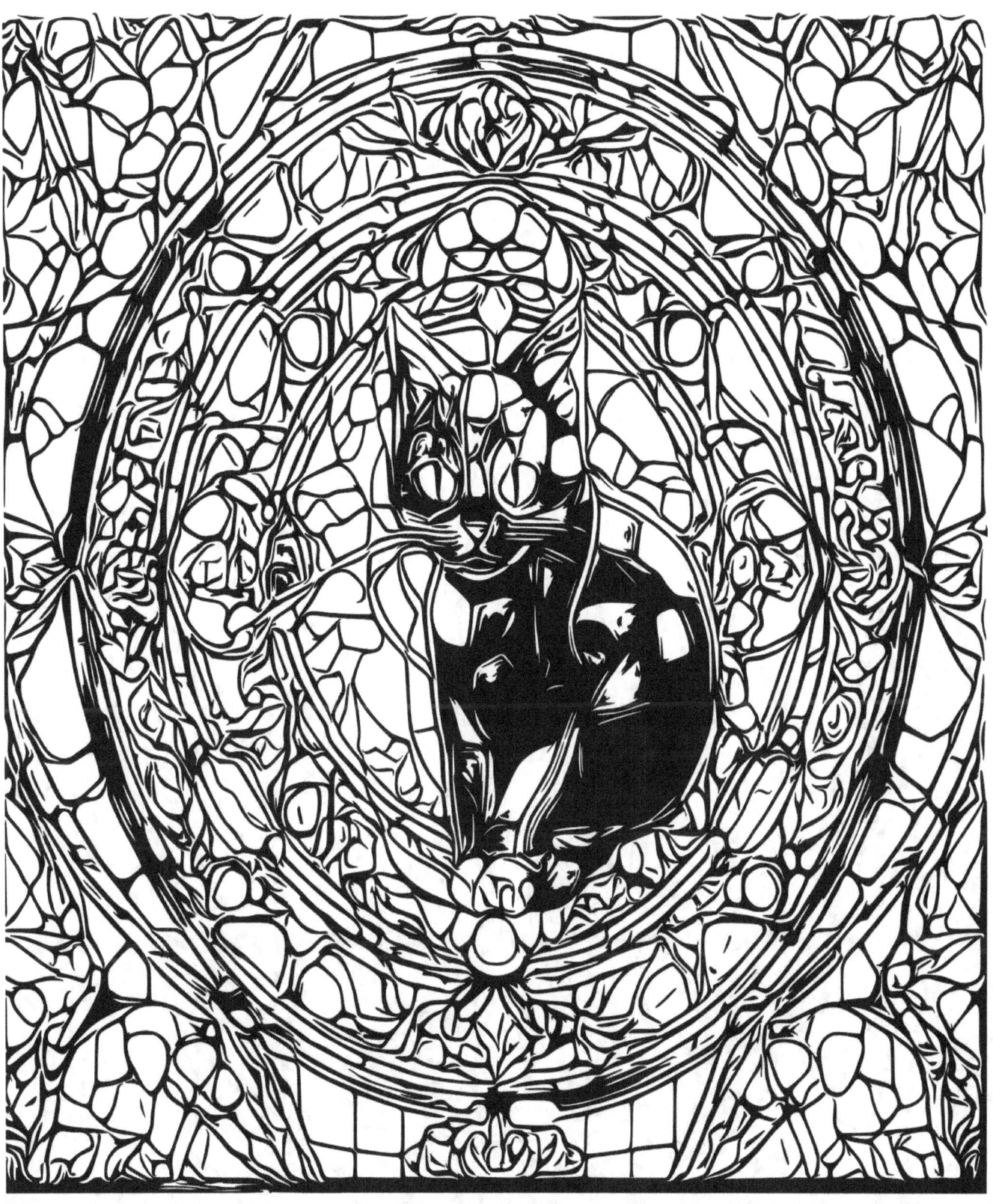

Black Cat 2

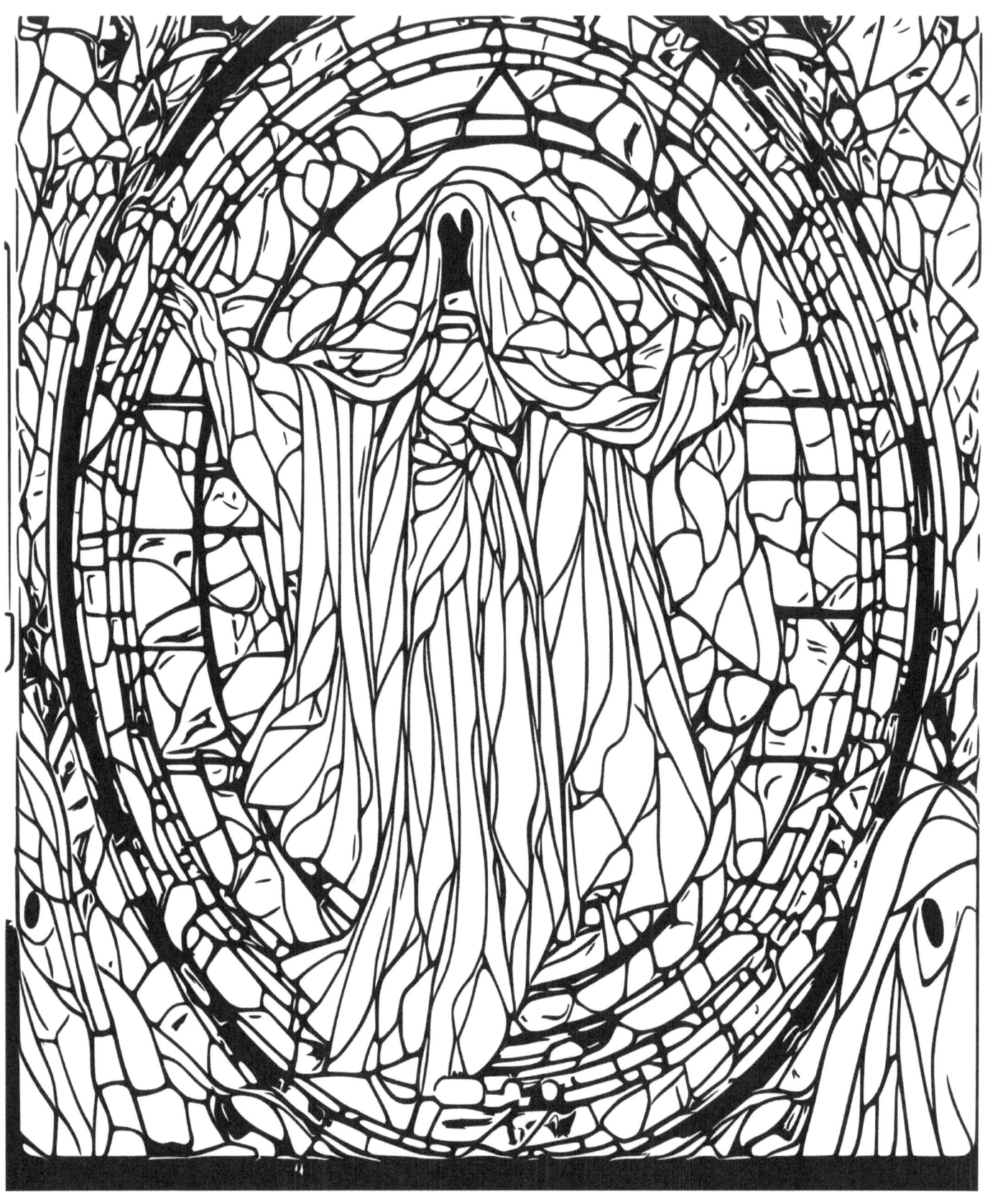

Ghost 1

October

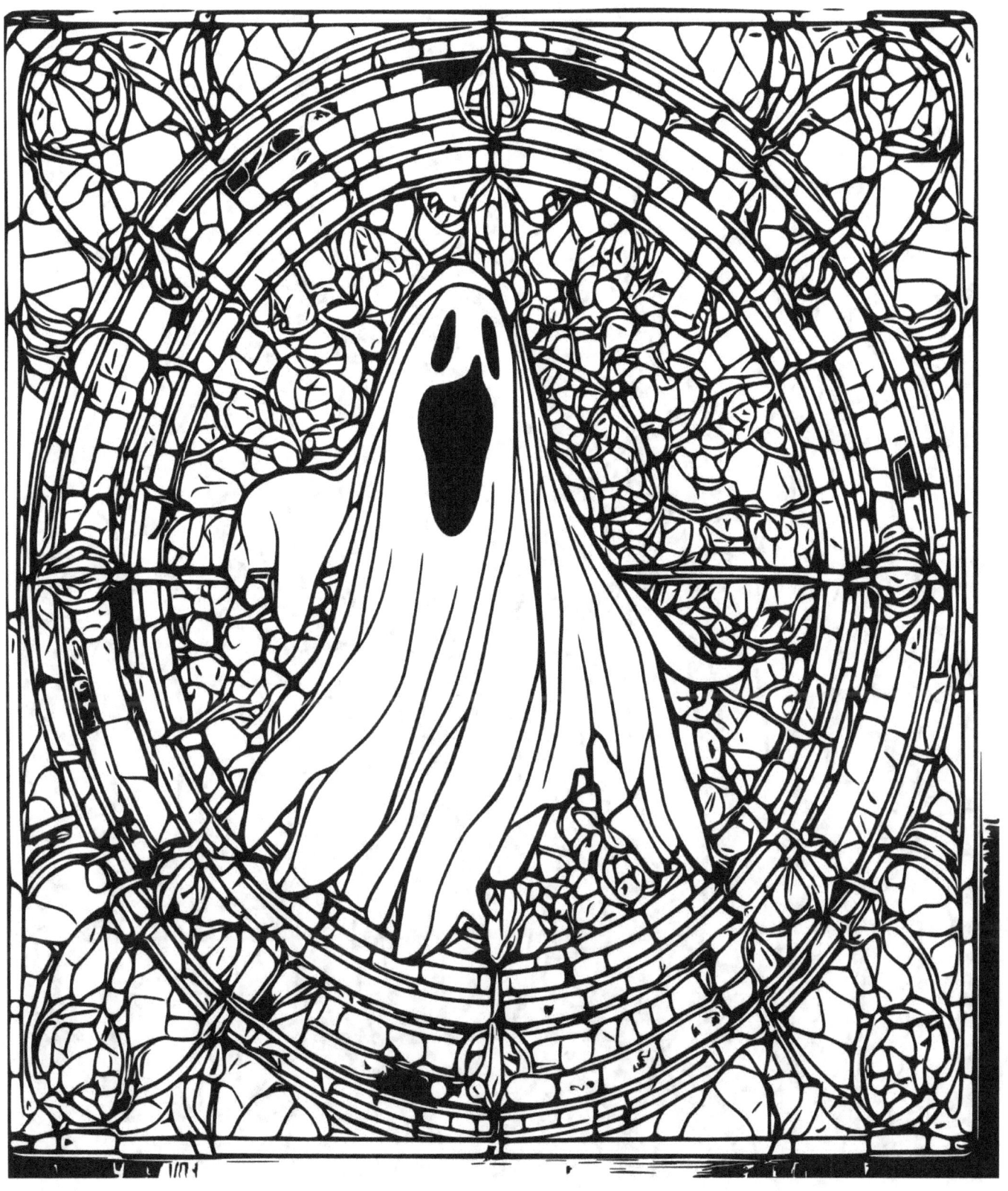

Ghost 2

October

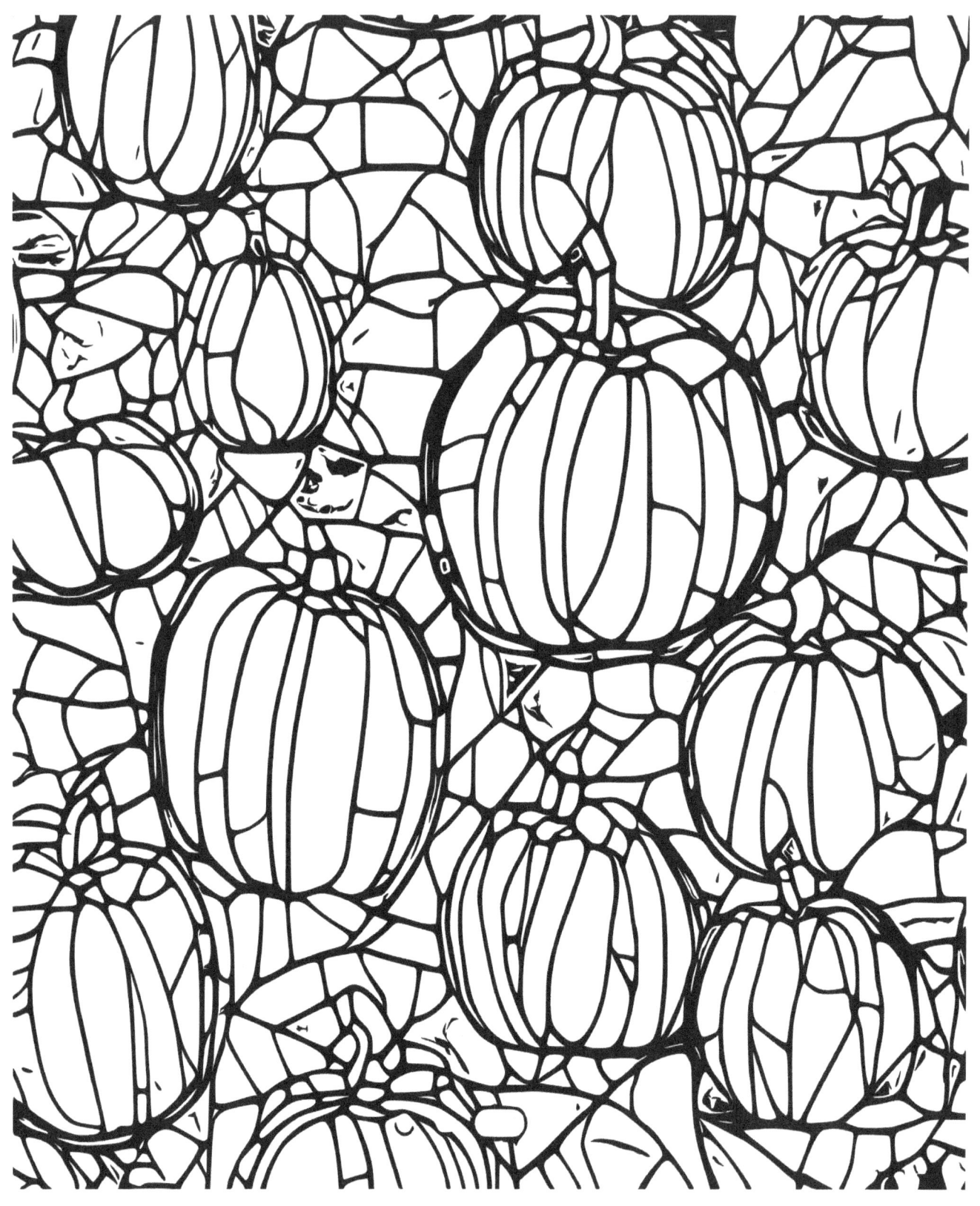

Pick a Pumpkin

October

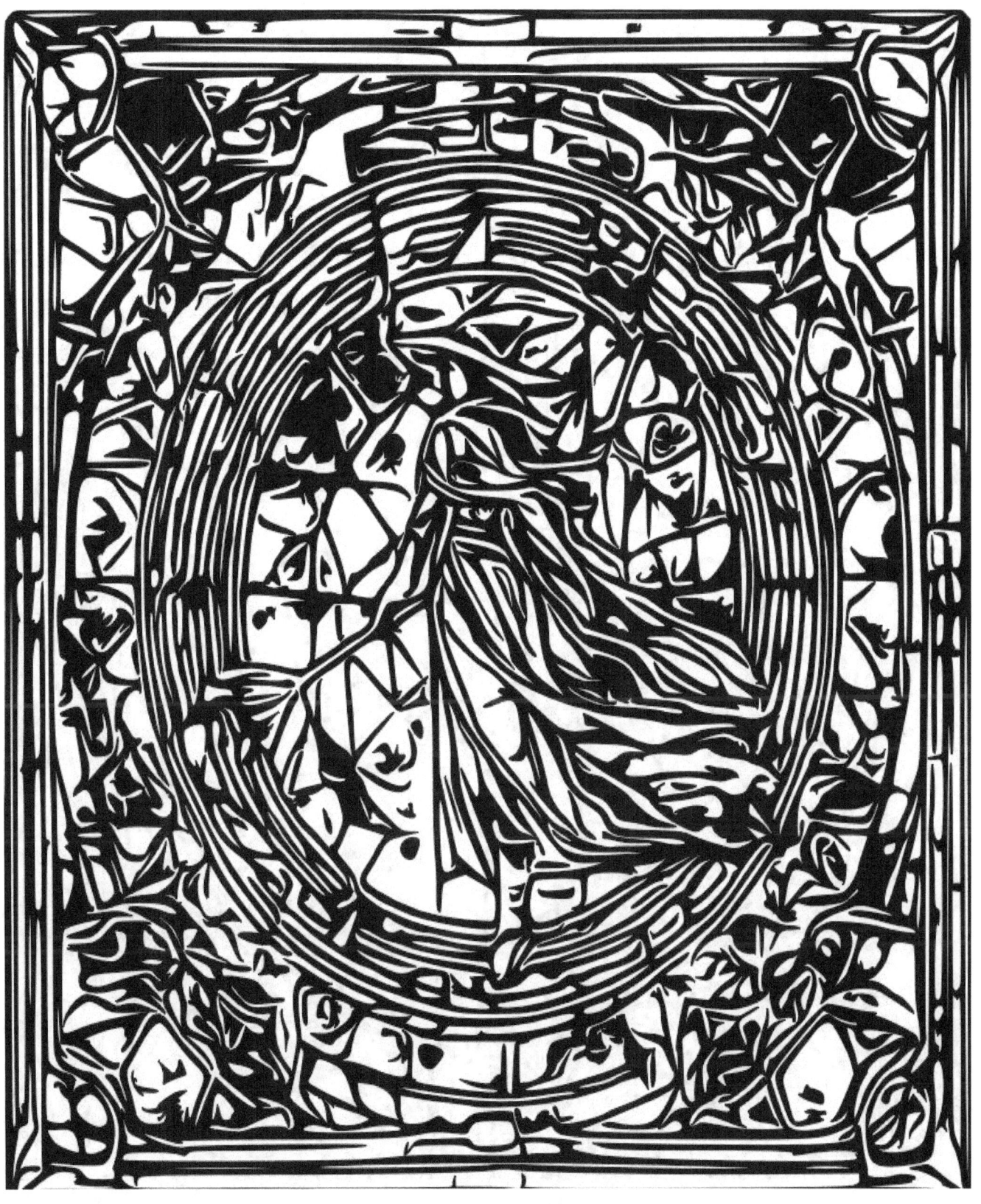

Witch with her Broomstick

November

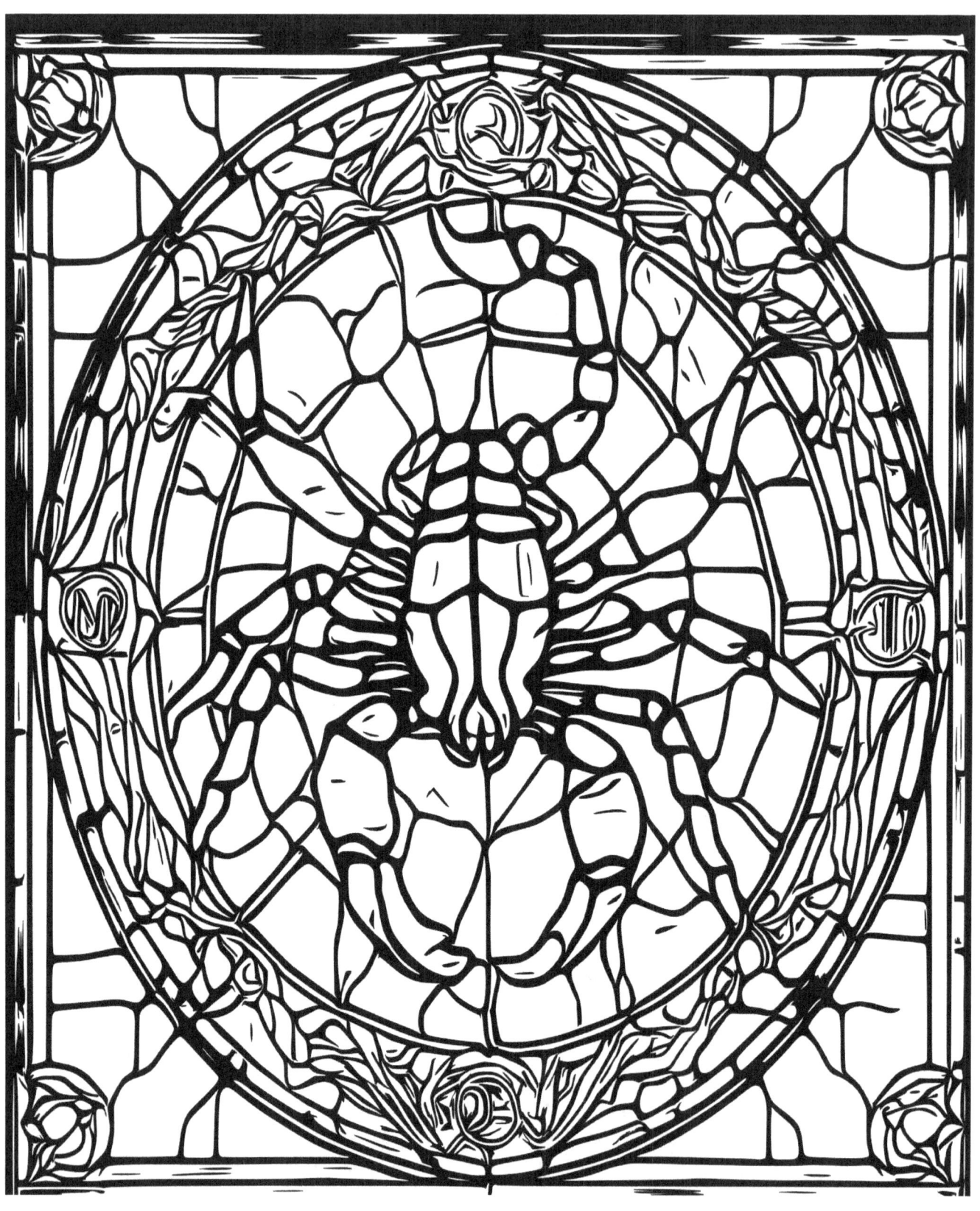

Scorpio

November

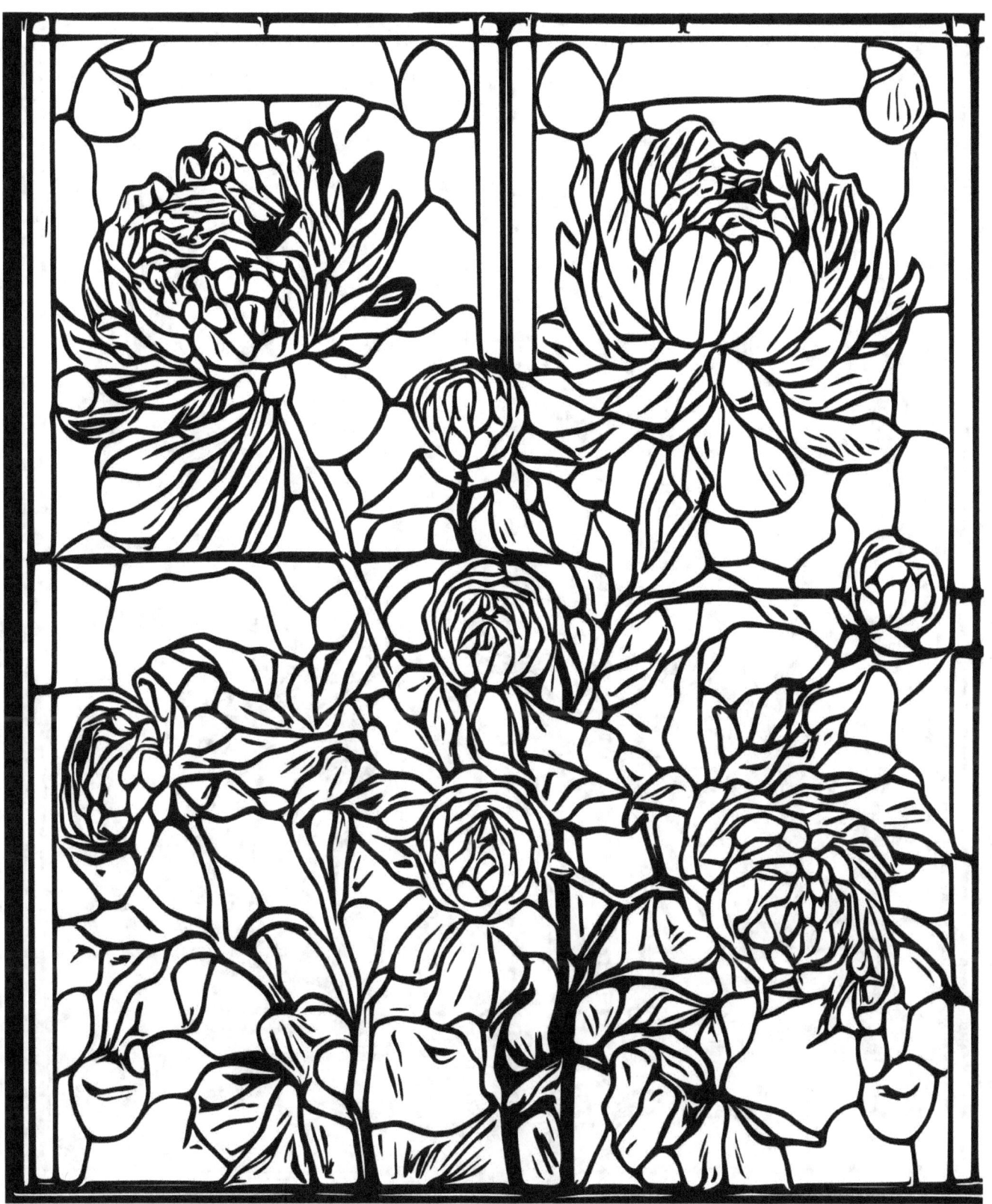

Flower of the Month: Chrysanthemum

November

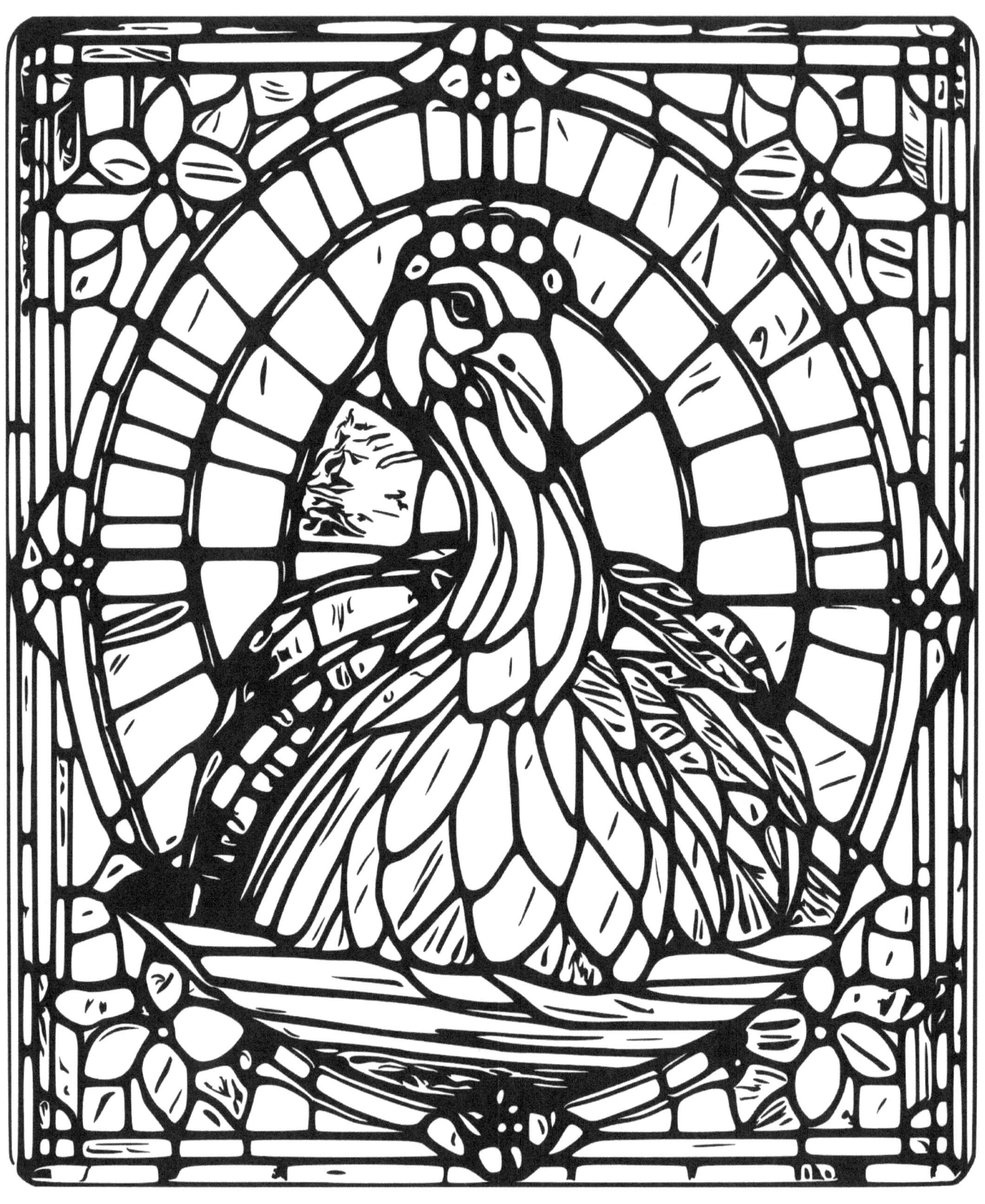

Turkey Day

November

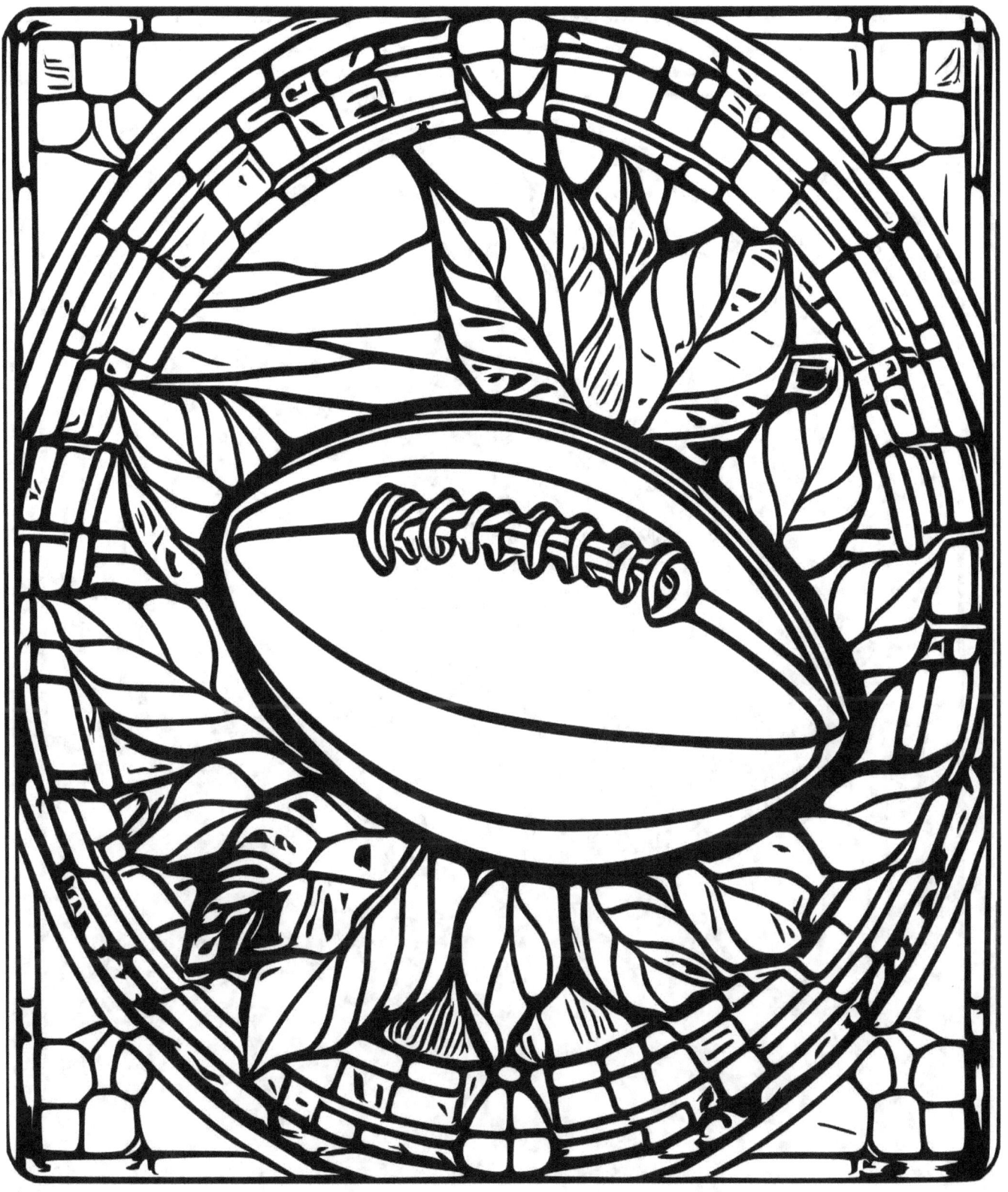

Football Season

November

The Copious Cornucopia

December

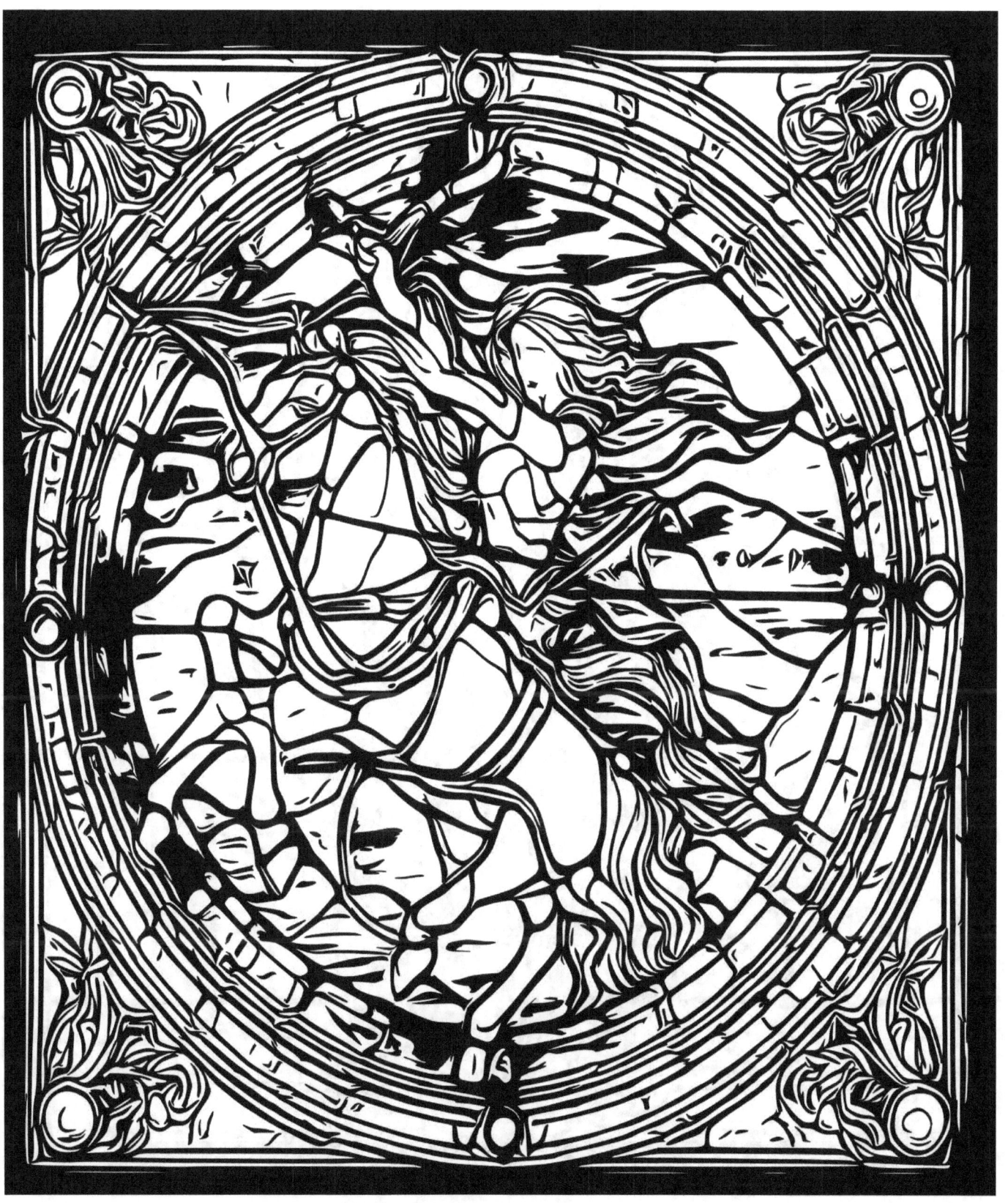

Sagittarius

December

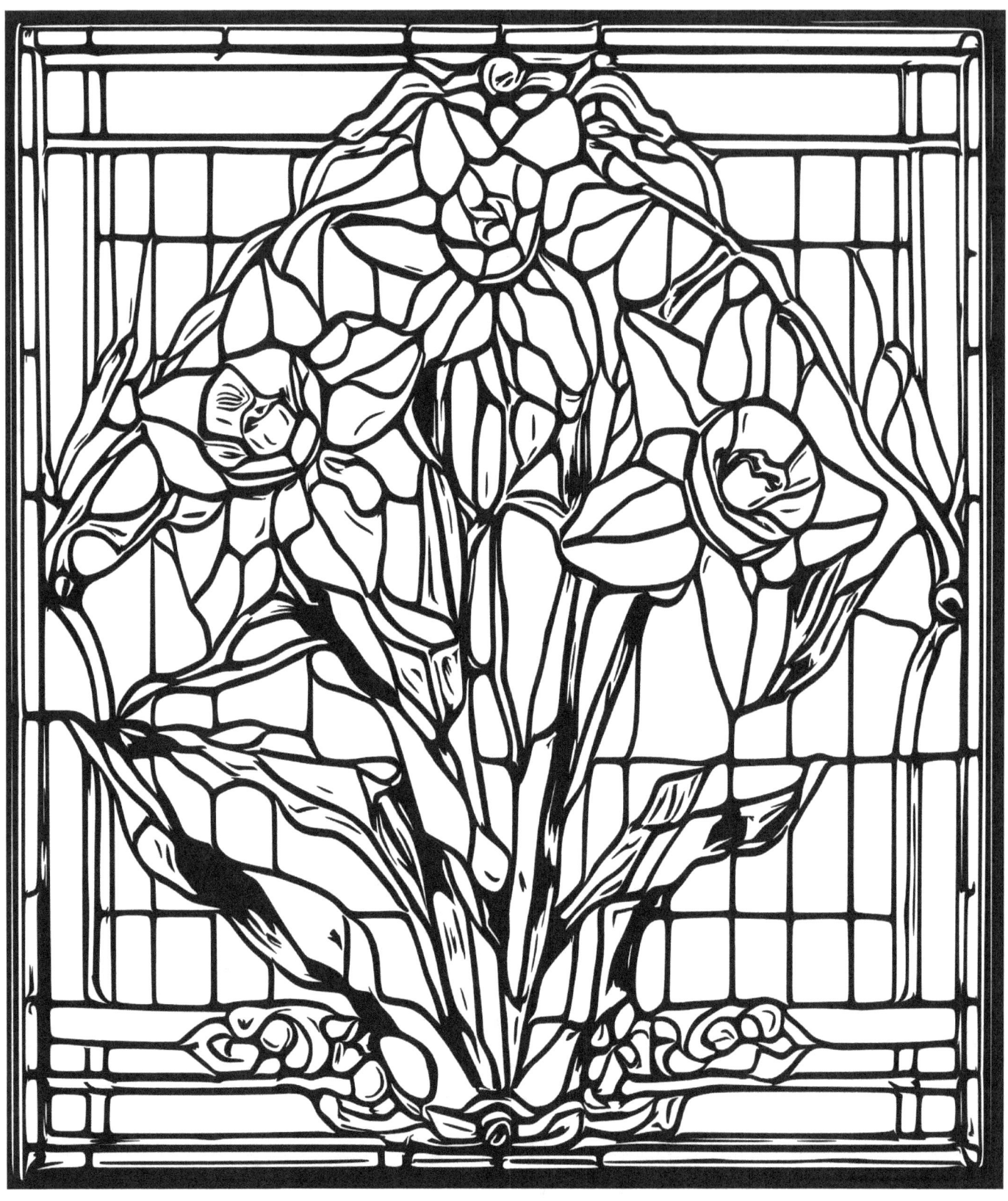

Flower of the Month: Narcissus

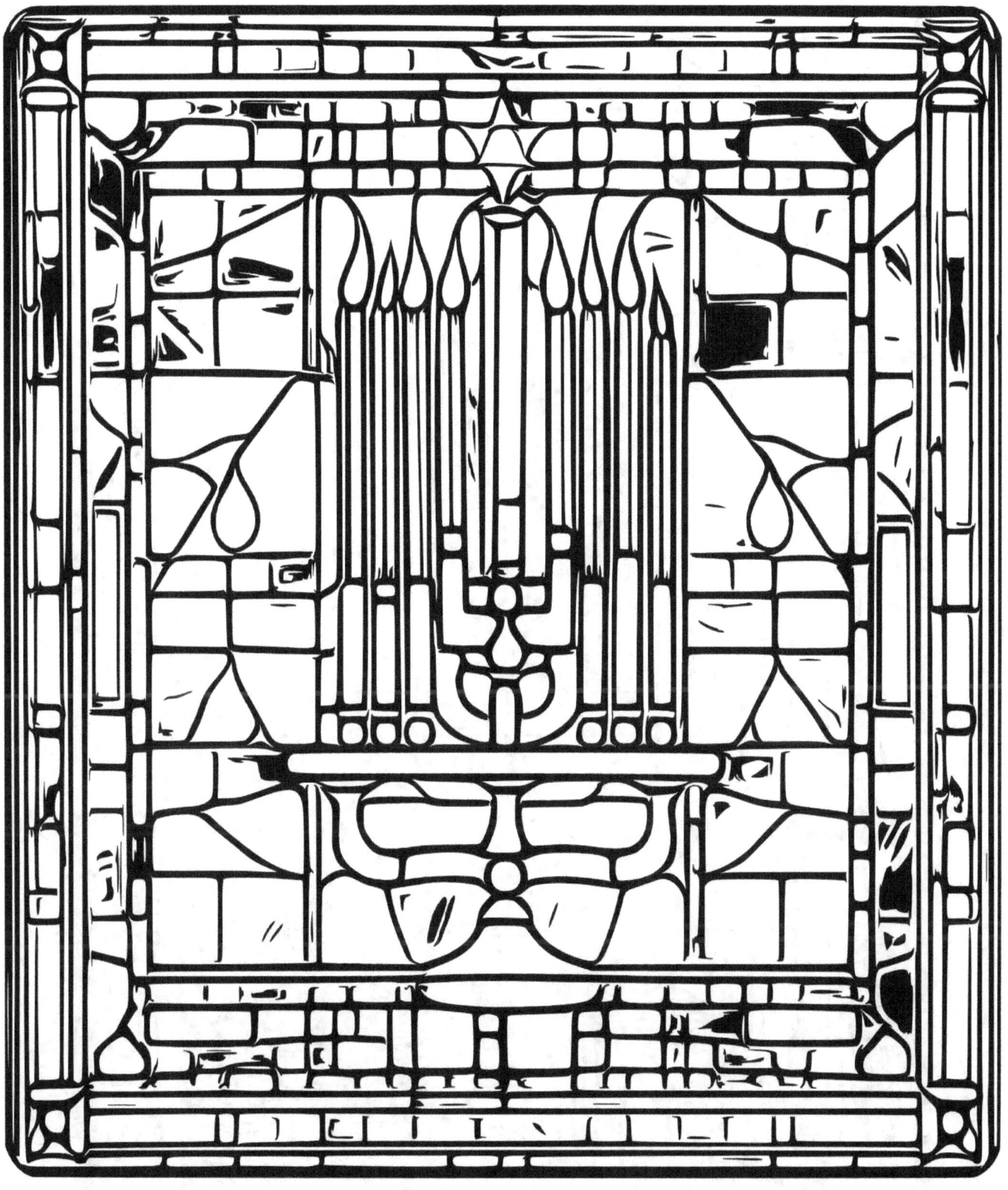

Hanukkah

December

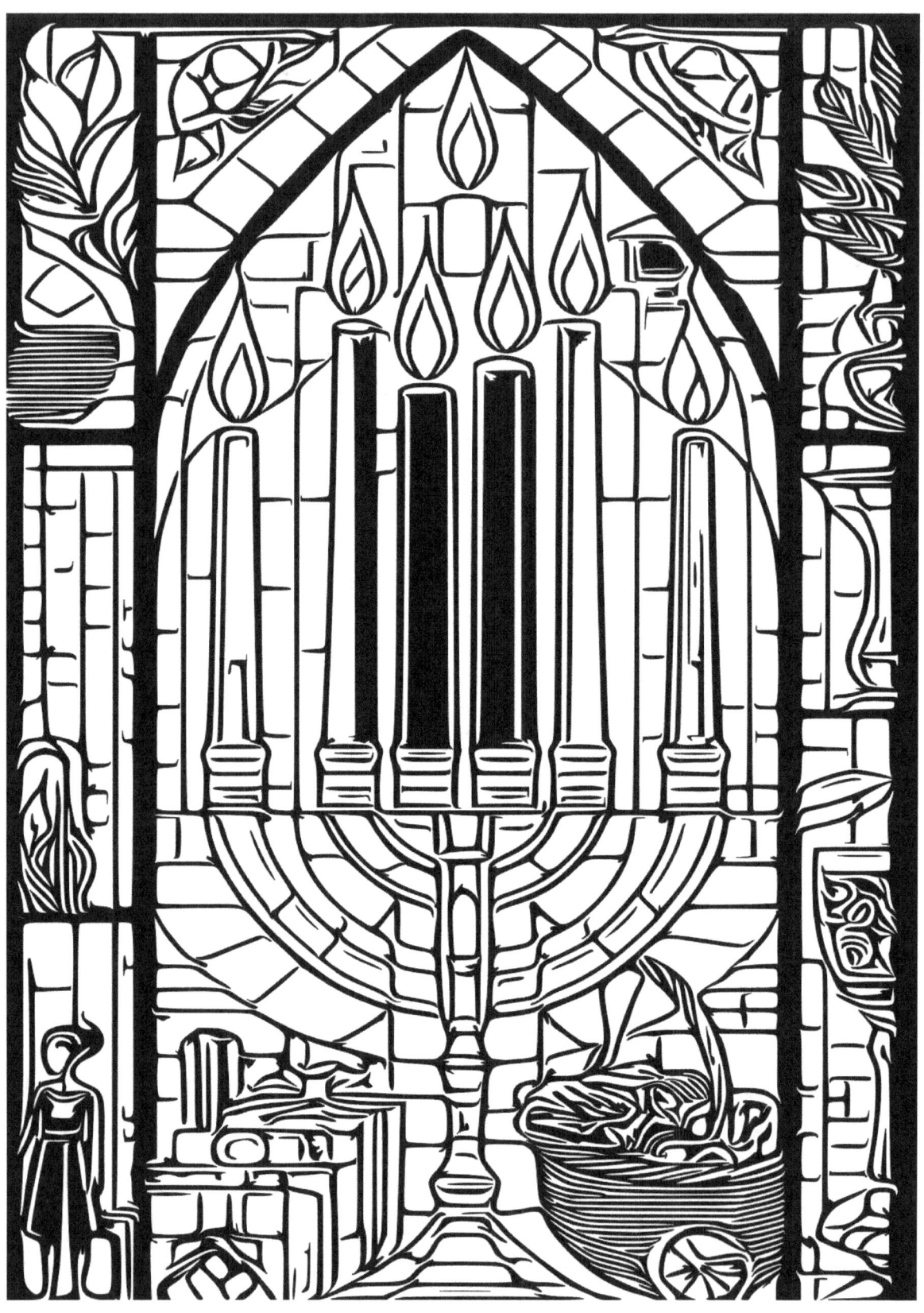

Kwanzaa

December

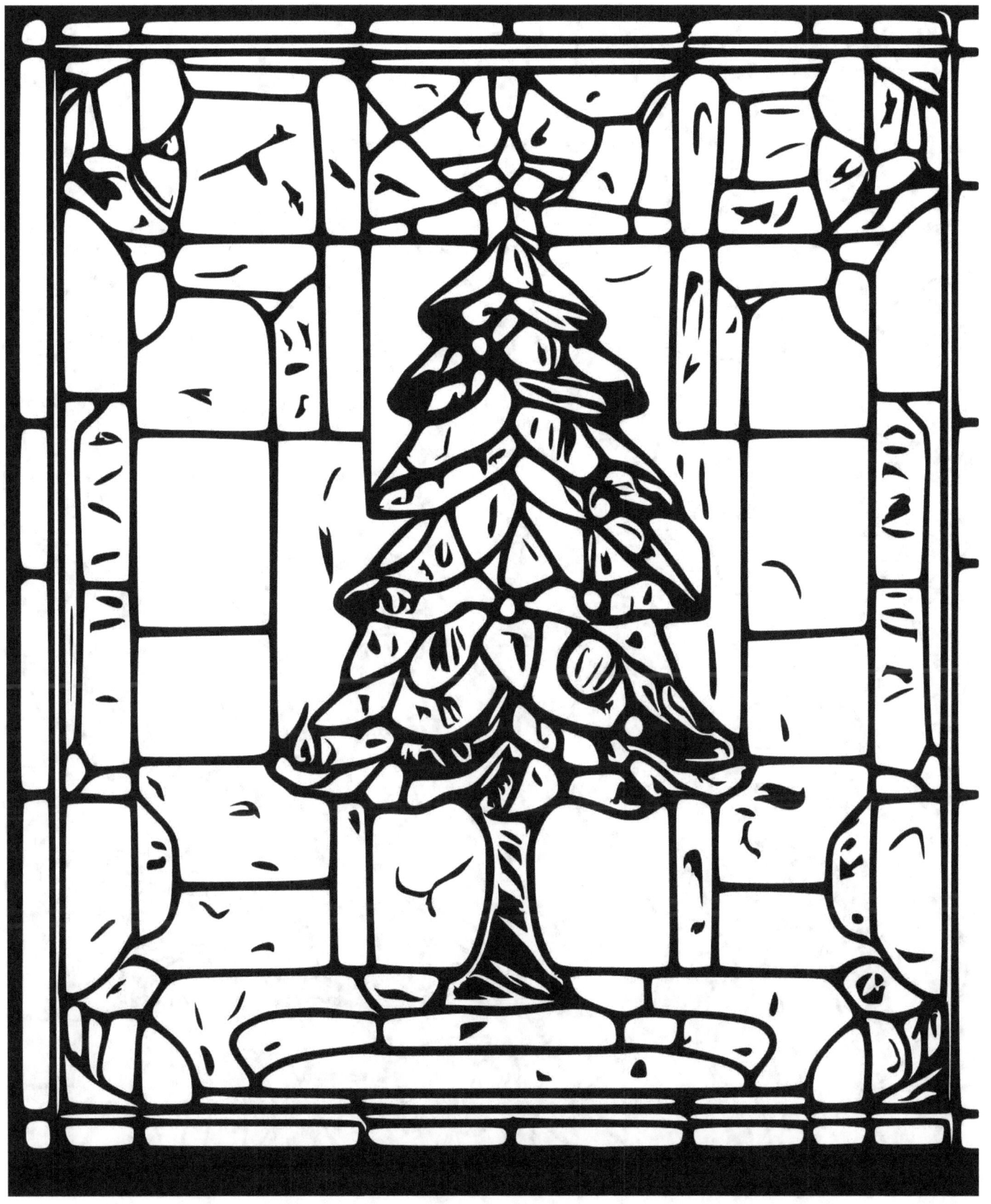

Christmas Tree

December

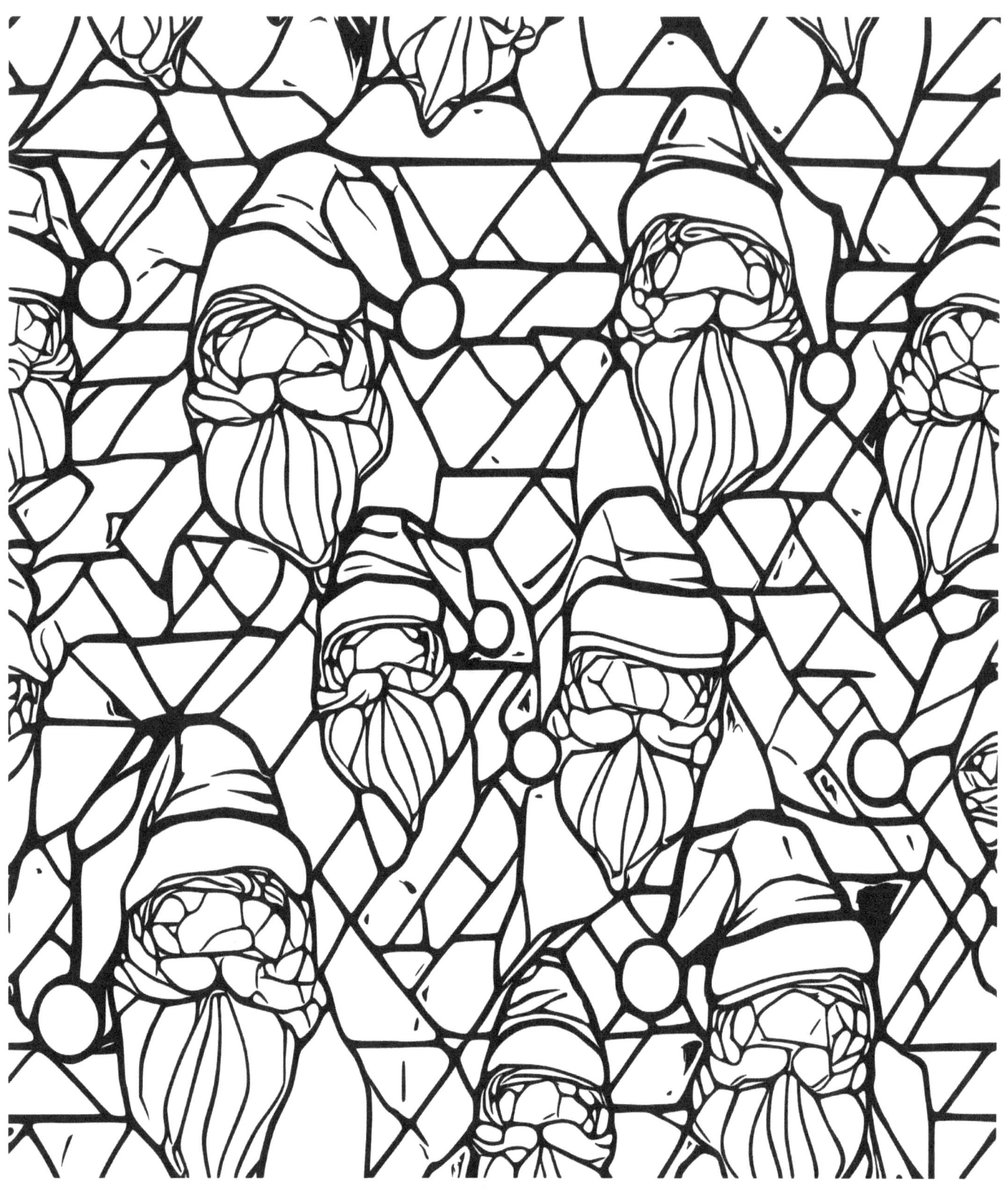

Santa's Watching

December

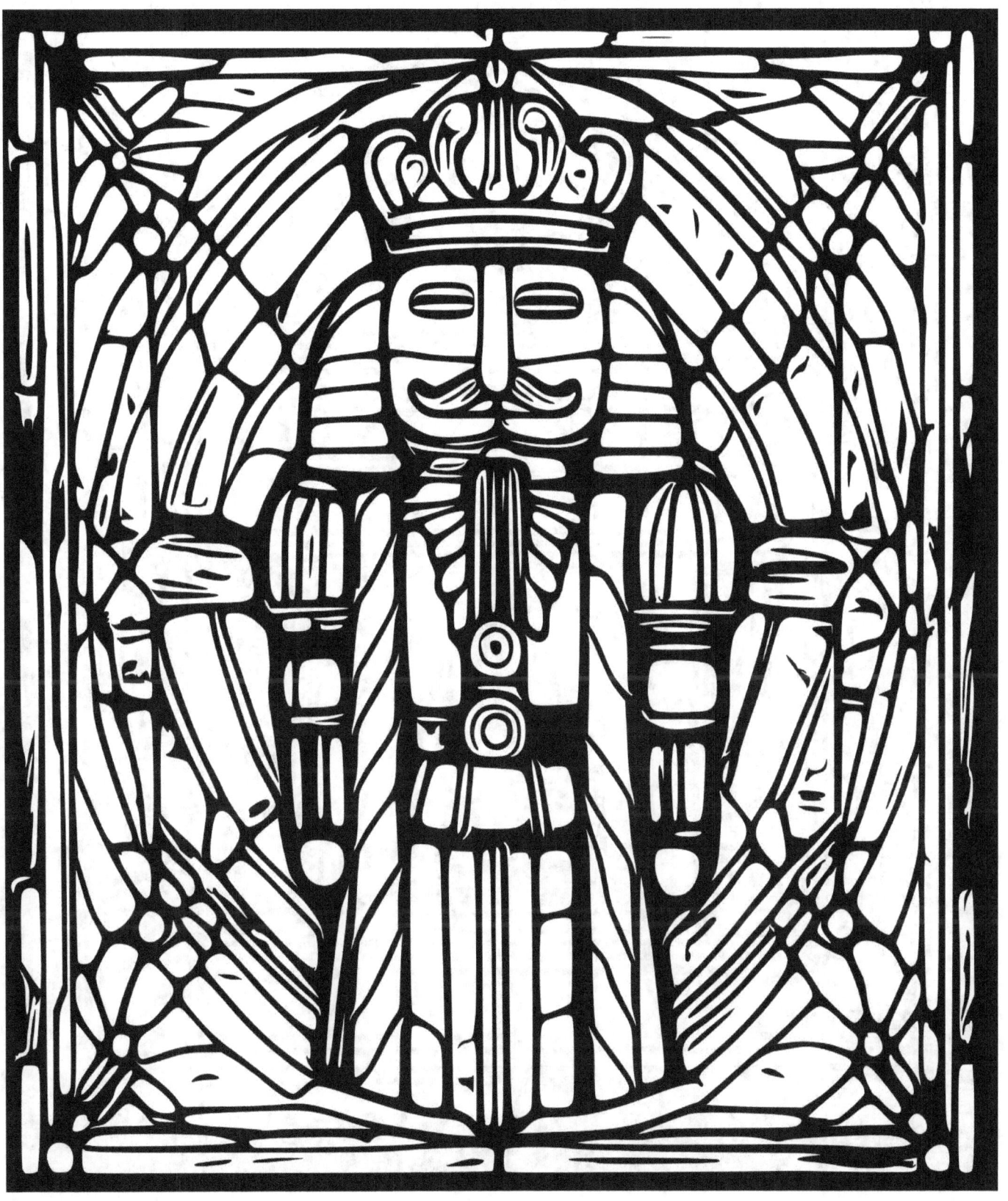

Nutcracker

December

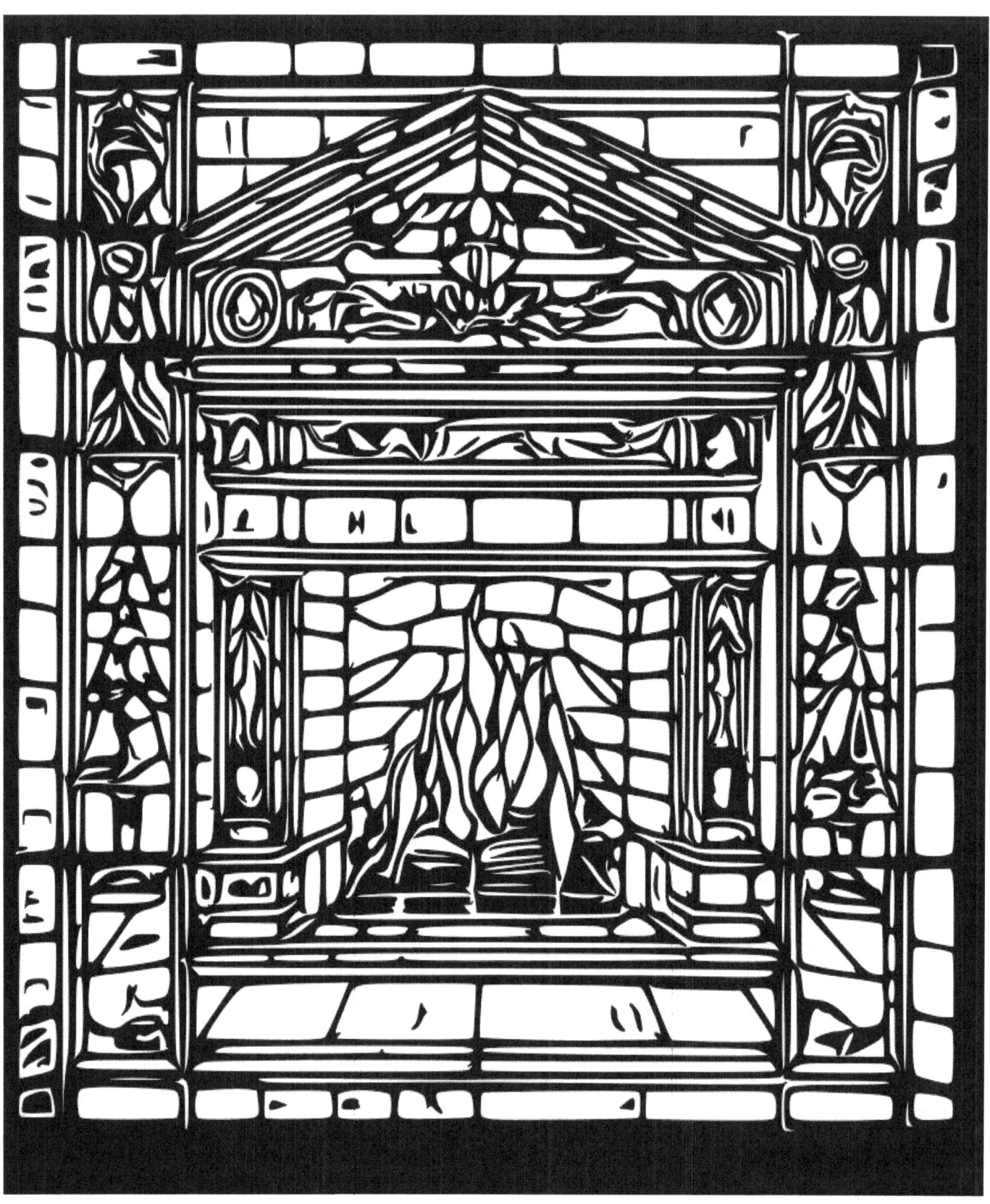

Warm by the Fireplace

www.ingramcontent.com/pod-product-compliance
Lightning Source LLC
Chambersburg PA
CBHW082225290526
45794CB00009B/3675